SCHOLASTIC

11+ PRACTICE PAPERS BOOK 1 AGES 10–11

T0382071

Prepare for the
GL 11+ TESTS
authentic multiple-choice papers

Maths

English

Verbal Reasoning

Non-verbal Reasoning

Published in the UK by Scholastic, 2022

Scholastic Education, Scholastic Distribution Centre,
Bosworth Avenue, Tournament Fields, Warwick CV34 6UQ

Scholastic Ireland, 89E Lagan Road, Dublin Industrial Estate,
Glasnevin, Dublin, D11 HP5F

SCHOLASTIC and associated logos are trademarks and/or
registered trademarks of Scholastic Inc.

© Scholastic, 2022

A CIP catalogue record for this book is available from the
British Library.

ISBN 978-0702-30888-8

Printed by Leo Paper Products, China.

The book is made of materials from well-managed,
FSC®-certified forests and other controlled sources.

4 5 6 7 8 9   4 5 6 7 8 9 0 1 2 3

Authors
Alison Milford and Nicola Palin

Editorial team
Rachel Morgan, Vicki Yates, Sarah Davies,
Julia Roberts and Jennie Clifford

Design team
Dipa Mistry and Justin Hoffmann, Couper Street Type Co.

Illustration
QBS Learning, Couper Street Type Co.

Contents

About the GL Assessment test

About the GL test

The Granada Learning (GL) Assessment is one of the leading providers of the tests that grammar schools use in selecting students at 11+. The GL Assessment test assesses students' ability in verbal reasoning, non-verbal reasoning, mathematics and English. Children typically take the GL Assessment test at the start of Year 6.

Students answer multiple-choice questions and record their answers on a separate answer sheet. This answer sheet is then marked via OMR (Optical Mark Recognition) scanning technology.

The structure and contents of the test can vary. Sometimes a separate paper is done per subject and sometimes papers are combined.

The English part of the test includes comprehension and spelling, punctuation and grammar questions. Verbal reasoning tends to include questions looking at word meanings, making words, relationships between numbers, and codes.

The mathematics tests are in line with the National Curriculum up to the start of Year 6. Questions will use knowledge of times tables, mental arithmetic, using the four operations, reading graphs, and shape, space and measure. Non-verbal reasoning focuses on processing graphic information, following patterns, applying maths skills (rotation, reflection, symmetry) and applying logical thinking and problem-solving skills.

The other main provider of 11+ tests is CEM. The CEM test assesses the same subjects as GL and uses a multiple-choice format.

About this book

Scholastic 11+ Practice Papers for the GL Assessment Test Ages 10–11 Book 1 is part of the *Pass Your 11+* series. The practice papers in this book have been designed to accurately reflect the format and style of the GL Assessment test.

The book offers:

- Two tests made up of two papers (Paper 1A and 1B and Paper 2A and 2B) to familiarise your child with the GL Assessment test
- Timings for each paper
- Multiple-choice questions to practise answering the types of question your child will meet in their GL Assessment test
- Multiple-choice answer sheets (in a centre section that can be pulled out for use). Printable answer sheets are also provided at www.scholastic.co.uk/pass-your-11-plus/extras/gl or via the QR code opposite
- Answers, including extended answers with explanations.

11+ Practice Paper 1A English and Verbal Reasoning

Information about this practice paper:

1. This paper is multiple choice. Mark your answer to each question in pencil on the answer sheet. Draw a firm line clearly through the rectangle on the answer sheet. If you make a mistake, rub it out and write in your new answer.

2. For pages 6–8, you have to read a text and then answer some questions about it. You can go back to the text to check your answers as many times as you want. There are also some spelling, punctuation and grammar exercises to do on pages 9–11.

3. Pages 12–17 have different types of questions. Each question starts with an explanation of what to do, followed by an example and solution with the answer marked on the answer sheet.

4. Some questions require more than one answer to be marked. Read the instructions carefully.

5. You may find some of the questions difficult. If you get stuck, **go to the next question**. If you are not sure, choose the answer you think is best.

6. **Work as quickly and as carefully as you can.**

You have 50 minutes to complete this paper.

English

Read the text and then answer the questions that follow on pages 7–8.

The Dragon's Pearl: A Retelling of an Ancient Chinese Myth

Long ago, in China, there was a terrible drought. Fertile fields of grass were now replaced with dry, scorched earth. Even the life-giving water of the River Min gradually diminished into muddy puddles.

In a riverside village, there lived a peasant boy and his mother. The drought had affected them badly and they were close to starvation. Every day, the boy would venture out to collect what little grass he
5   could find and then sell it in exchange for money. With this, he could just about buy a bowl of rice to feed him and his mother.

On one hot day, the boy found himself walking further from his village in a desperate search for better-quality grass. When he passed a large rock, he noticed a soft, green glow seeping through the end of a narrow crevice. Filled with curiosity, the boy tentatively squeezed through the gap, only to
10   find himself standing on a luxurious carpet of green grass! With renewed strength, he cut it down and rushed back to the village. That night, he and his mother ate well.

The next day, the boy retraced his steps, in the hope of finding more fresh grass. To his astonishment, it had miraculously regrown on the same patch he had cut the day before! That night, he and his mother ate more food than they had in a year.

15   Day after day, the boy visited the same place to cut the thick grass that regrew there every night. After a while he began to tire of his daily trek and decided to dig up the grass's roots and replant them by his home. As the boy dug into the soil, a smooth, round object caught his eye; it was an exquisite pearl.

With the grass in his basket and the pearl in his pocket, he ran home as fast as he could. His mother was utterly enchanted by the pearl's beauty and immediately placed it inside a rice sack for safekeeping.

20   Next morning, the boy was distraught to discover that his grass had withered away. "I have ruined our good luck by being lazy," he cried out. His mother disagreed. "The pearl has brought us luck!" she laughed, and she pointed at the rice flowing from the sack.

From then on, large amounts of food would magically appear. Being kind people, the boy and his mother shared their prosperity with the rest of the grateful villagers. But a few greedy villagers coveted
25   the pearl for themselves.

One hot afternoon, they demanded the boy hand over the magic pearl. "Never!" screamed the boy, and he swallowed it! Immediately, the boy felt an intense burning in his stomach. "I need water," he gasped. He raced down to the parched river and guzzled up what little water was there. Just at that moment, there was a loud clap of thunder, and a deluge of rain poured down from the skies. The rough
30   cracks in the soil merged together like old friends greeting each other, the withered crops straightened their backs to enjoy an energising shower and the villagers danced with joy.

However, all the boy's mother could do was weep, for something remarkable was happening to her beloved son. As the water flowed, his body changed into a long serpentine form, covered in emerald-green scales; razor-sharp teeth appeared in his wide mouth and his eyes became fiery orange
35   discs. The boy had transformed into a mighty river dragon.

With the glowing pearl placed under its chin, the dragon flapped its gigantic wings and flew into the sky. From that time on, it was said that the river dragon protected the land from natural disasters so that people would not starve again.

Answer the questions about the text on page 6. Mark your answers on the answer sheet on page 33.

1   How had the drought affected the boy and his mother?

    A   They moved to another village.

    B   They were close to starvation.

    C   They became mean to their neighbours.

    D   They began to steal food from a local farm.

    E   They grew vegetables in their garden.

2   Why did the boy walk further away from the village?

    A   To search for a fresh source of water

    B   To have some time alone

    C   To find fresh green grass

    D   To get fitter

    E   To collect fresh fruit and vegetables

3   Which of the following words best describes the boy?

    A   thoughtful

    B   angry

    C   selfish

    D   bored

    E   nervous

4   What was special about the pearl?

    A   It belonged to an extraordinarily rich emperor.

    B   It granted three wishes.

    C   It turned everything green.

    D   It was a dragon's egg.

    E   It increased things wherever it was placed.

5   Which of the following statements is NOT true?

    A   Some villagers attempted to steal the pearl.

    B   The boy felt like his stomach was burning.

    C   The boy put the pearl in his mouth and swallowed it.

    D   The mother threw the pearl into a well.

    E   All the water left in the river was drunk by the boy.

6 'The rough cracks in the soil merged together like old friends greeting each other'. (lines 29–30)

This phrase contains an example of:

A simile

B metaphor

C alliteration

D analogy

E onomatopoeia

7 **What did people believe the river dragon did next?**

A It hid in the highest mountains.

B It burned down all the fields and villages.

C It caused storms and floods.

D It drank all the rivers dry.

E It protected their land from natural disasters.

Answer this question about the meaning of words in the text on page 6. Mark your answers on the answer sheet on page 33.

8 **Which word is closest in meaning to 'tentatively'? (line 9)**

A confidently

B carefully

C quietly

D quickly

E unwillingly

Answer this question about words and phrases as they are used in the text on page 6. Mark your answers on the answer sheet on page 33.

9 **'Even the life-giving water of the River Min gradually diminished into muddy puddles.' (line 2)**

Which word is a verb?

A River Min

B muddy

C life-giving

D diminished

E even

Anni's Rainforest

This text has some punctuation or capital letter mistakes. On each numbered line there is either one mistake or no mistake. Find the group of words containing the mistake and mark the letter of the group on the answer sheet. If there is no mistake, then select 'N'. Mark your answers on the answer sheet on page 33.

1   Sinchi's brash city-talk was beginning to get on anni's nerves. Quickly and quietly,
       A   B   C   D

2   she crept towards the one place where she felt truly at peace – the rainforest.
       A   B   C   D

3   However, Sinchi was on full alert. he had no desire to be stuck in
       A   B   C   D

4   his cousins village. "Hey, wait!" he yelled as Anni disappeared into
       A   B   C   D

5   the dark trees. "I want to find out why you like the forest so much"
       A   B   C   D

6   With a sigh of resignation Anni led Sinchi carefully through the steamy
       A   B   C   D

7   forest, full of colour and noise. "What a dump?" exclaimed Sinchi. "It's just a
       A   B   C   D

8   noisy smelly wood!" Anni glared at Sinchi in anger. "The rainforest is a
       A   B   C   D

9   very special habitat. Hundreds of plants and creatures wouldnt survive without it."
       A   B   C   D

Dear Diary

This text has some spelling mistakes. In each numbered line there is either one spelling mistake or no mistake. Find the group of words containing the mistake and mark the letter of the group on the answer sheet. If there is no mistake, then select 'N'. Mark your answers on the answer sheet on page 33.

1   I'm having a great time on our residential trip and today was no exception! This morning,
       A   B   C   D

2   we visited the ruins of a Roman fought on Hadrian's Wall. The local guide told us
       A   B   C   D

3   about the famous legend of the lost Ninth Roman Lejun. It seems that they
       A   B   C   D

4   marched off to carry out their daily patroll and were never seen again. They
       A   B   C   D

5   disappeared into thin air. Then, just as we were walking back to our coach, we
       A   B   C   D

6   heard a stedy drum beat and the clanging of metal. Marching straight towards us,
       A   B   C   D

7   were some Roman soldiers. We couldn't beleive our eyes; the lost legion had returned!
       A   B   C   D

8   However, we soon realised that they were actualy college students doing
       A   B   C

   a sponsored walk!
       D

Night Terror

Choose a word or group of words to complete the passage so that it makes sense and uses correct English. Mark the letter underneath your chosen word or words on the answer sheet on page 33.

1   Fred [seated] [sat] [sitted] [has sit] [sitting] bolt upright.
         A   B   C   D   E

2   Something [had woke] [has woked] [is waking] [had woken] [has woke] him up,
                  A   B   C   D   E

3   but he wasn't sure what it [was] [is] [were] [am] [are].
                                 A   B   C   D   E

4   [However] [Whereas] [Despite] [As well as] [Unusually] being cocooned in a warm bed,
        A   B   C   D   E

5   Fred [shouldn't] [might not] [hasn't] [oughtn't] [couldn't] stop shivering.
            A   B   C   D   E

6   A dark shape flittered [between] [across] [next to] [in] [above] the ceiling.
                              A   B   C   D   E

7   In terror, Fred [trys] [is trying] [has tried] [tried] [managed] to scream for help
                      A   B   C   D   E

8   but nothing would come out of [his] [our] [her] [their] [its] mouth.
                                     A   B   C   D   E

Verbal Reasoning

In questions 1–4, a **four-letter word** is hidden at the **end** of one word and the **start** of the next word.

Find the two words that contain the hidden word. Mark your answers on the answer sheet on page 33.

Example: Mia bought a comb and brush.

Mia bought	bought a	a comb	comb and	and brush.
A	B	C	D	E

Answer: **comb and**

Solution: The hidden word is **band**: Mia bought a com**b and** brush.

---

1 Listen to the patter of rain.

Listen to	to the	the patter	patter of	of rain.
A	B	C	D	E

2 Have you got any yellow ink?

Have you	you got	got any	any yellow	yellow ink?
A	B	C	D	E

3 The thief grabbed gems with diamonds.

The thief	thief grabbed	grabbed gems	gems with	with diamonds.
A	B	C	D	E

4 The puffin dived off the cliff.

The puffin	puffin dived	dived off	off the	the cliff.
A	B	C	D	E

In questions 1–5, choose the **two** words, one from each group, that will help the sentences make sense. Mark **both** words on the answer sheet on page 34.

Example: **Short** is to (tall happy green) as **low** is to (table red high).

A	tall		**X**	table
B	happy		**Y**	red
C	green		**Z**	high

Answer: **tall high**

Solution: **Tall** is the antonym of **short**. **High** is the antonym of **low**.

---

1   **Ocean** is to (grass wet arid) as **desert** is to (dry hot sand).

A	grass		**X**	dry
B	wet		**Y**	hot
C	arid		**Z**	sand

2   **Jupiter** is to (rocket hero planet) as **Sun** is to (star hot holiday).

A	rocket		**X**	star
B	hero		**Y**	hot
C	planet		**Z**	holiday

3   **Minute** is to (time month day) as **metre** is to (heavy length shape).

A	time		**X**	heavy
B	month		**Y**	length
C	day		**Z**	shape

4   **Buttons** is to (shirt hat belt) as **laces** is to (scarf shoes collar).

A	shirt		**X**	scarf
B	hat		**Y**	shoes
C	belt		**Z**	collar

5   **Stroll** is to (swim walk fast) as **sprint** is to (run slow kick).

A	swim		**X**	run
B	walk		**Y**	slow
C	fast		**Z**	kick

Find the letters that will help the sentences in questions 1–5 make sense.

Use the alphabet below to help you. Mark your answers on the answer sheet on page 34.

A B C D E F G H I J K L M N O P Q R S T U V W X Y Z

Example: **AB** is to **CD** as **MN** is to [?]

        A OQ   **B** OP   **C** KL   **D** PQ   **E** NO

Answer: **OP**

Solution: The letters **CD** come after **AB**. The two letters after **MN** are **OP**.

---

1   **DW** is to **EV** as **FU** is to [?]

        A GT   **B** CX   **C** BY   **D** HS   **E** AZ

2   **BD** is to **GI** as **LN** is to [?]

        A EG   **B** MO   **C** QS   **D** QT   **E** OP

3   **MQ** is to **NP** as **VZ** is to [?]

        A XZ   **B** WY   **C** UY   **D** VT   **E** US

4   **HD** is to **BA** as **WS** is to [?]

        A QP   **B** UW   **C** RP   **D** SP   **E** XY

5   **ML** is to **KG** as **VU** is to [?]

        A TP   **B** KM   **C** TR   **D** TW   **E** RN

In questions 1–5, the **three** words in the second set go together in the **same way** as the three words in the first set.

Find the missing word in the second set. Mark your answers on the answer sheet on page 34.

Example:	(pan [pat] tug) (hop [?] ten)
	A hot **B** ten **C** top **D** pen **E** hen
Answer:	hot
Solution:	The word 'pat' is made from the first and second letters in 'pan' and the first letter in 'tug'.

1   (skin [kid] damp)   (drum [?] bend)

        A red   **B** mend   **C** rub   **D** bed   **E** dub

2   (loan [list] mist)   (wish [?] land)

        A hand   **B** lash   **C** wind   **D** wish   **E** wand

3   (table [blow] grow)   (straw [?] cling)

        A rang   **B** sing   **C** wing   **D** sung   **E** ring

4   (crumb [crush] shelf)   (creak [?] ample)

        A cramp   **B** cream   **C** clamp   **D** crepe   **E** creep

5   (class [cage] green)   (main [?] cress)

        A mess   **B** nice   **C** mass   **D** mice   **E** acre

In questions 1–4, find **two** words, one from each group, that are **closest in meaning**.

Mark **both** words on the answer sheet on page 34.

Example: (cook mix divide)   (blend paint friendly)

        A   cook   X   blend

        B   mix   Y   paint

        C   divide   Z   friendly

Answer: **mix blend**

Solution: Both **mix** and **blend** can mean combining things together.

---

1   (reply share explain)   (letter answer ask)

      A   reply   X   letter

      B   share   Y   answer

      C   explain   Z   ask

2   (dangerous energy delicate)   (fragile strong safe)

      A   dangerous   X   fragile

      B   energy   Y   strong

      C   delicate   Z   safe

3   (spectator athlete driver)   (instructor singer observer)

      A   spectator   X   instructor

      B   athlete   Y   singer

      C   driver   Z   observer

4   (solid flexible difficult)   (bendy round liquid)

      A   solid   X   bendy

      B   flexible   Y   round

      C   difficult   Z   liquid

In questions 1–5, find the number that continues the series in the best way.

Mark your answers on the answer sheet on page 34.

Example: 3   5   7   9   [?]

      A 10   B 11   C 13   D 18   E 16

Answer: **11**

Solution: It is a sequence of odd numbers.

---

1   5   9   13   17   [?]

    A 21   B 20   C 19   D 22   E 30

2   16   12   8   4   8   12   [?]

    A 14   B 8   C 16   D 4   E 13

3   72   101   80   109   88   [?]

    A 100   B 94   C 110   D 117   E 84

4   12   11   14   13   16   15   18   [?]

    A 17   B 19   C 20   D 21   E 16

5   38   16   36   18   34   20   32   [?]

    A 30   B 21   C 22   D 28   E 34

Read the information below, then work out the answer to the question. Mark your answer on the answer sheet on page 34.

1   Josh, Meena, Isla and Dan all go to the theme park.
        Josh, Isla and Dan go on the rollercoaster.
        Dan goes down the water slide.
        Meena goes on the big wheel and down the water slide.
        Isla sees the ghost house ride but does not go on it.
        Josh and Meena have fun driving the dodgem cars.

    Who does the fewest things in the theme park?

    A Meena   B Dan   C Isla   D Josh

11+ Practice Paper 1B Mathematics and Non-verbal Reasoning

Information about this practice paper:

1. This paper is multiple choice. Mark your answer to each question in pencil on the answer sheet beginning on page 35. Draw a firm line clearly through the rectangle on the answer sheet. If you make a mistake, rub it out and write in your new answer.

2. Pages 19–24 contain mathematics questions. Read all of the questions carefully.

3. Pages 25–30 contain two different picture-based question types. Each question starts with an explanation of what to do, followed by an example and the solution with the answer marked on the answer sheet.

4. You may find some of the questions difficult. If you get stuck, **go to the next question**. If you are not sure, choose the answer you think is best.

5. **Work as quickly and as carefully as you can.**

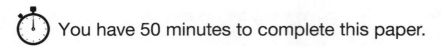 You have 50 minutes to complete this paper.

Mathematics

Mark your answers to the following questions on the answer sheet on page 35.

1 Four hundred and thirteen thousand six hundred and seven

How is this number written in digits?

A 41,367 **B** 430,607 **C** 413,600.7 **D** 413,670 **E** 413,607

2 **How much water will be left in the jug if 0.2 l is poured out?**

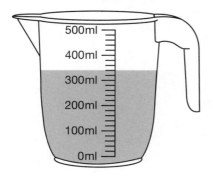

A 140ml **B** 320ml **C** 120ml **D** 240ml **E** 540ml

3 **Which statement is correct?**

A 47,256 > 47,265

B 63,629 < 62,693

C 24,214 > 24,124

D 82,502 < 80,255

E 19,347 < 18,437

4 **Which answer correctly completes the sentence?**

The sum of three odd numbers will always

A end in 3. **B** be odd. **C** be a multiple of 3. **D** end in 5. **E** be even.

5   **Which number is a multiple of 6 and 8?**

   A 18   **B** 22   **C** 36   **D** 42   **E** 72

---

6   William bought seven apples and some pears. He paid £6.25 in total.

   How many pears did he buy?

apples	55p each
pears	40p each

   A 4   **B** 5   **C** 6   **D** 7   **E** 8

---

7   **Which year is written in Roman numerals as MMXII?**

   A 2007   **B** 212   **C** 2120   **D** 2012   **E** 2002

---

8   **What is the first term in this sequence?**

   ____ ____ 121   274   427

   A −185   **B** 12   **C** −147   **D** −427   **E** −72

---

9   These temperatures were recorded in January.

   Which city has the greatest difference between its day and night temperatures?

City	Day temperature	Night temperature
Ottawa	−6°C	−14°C
Moscow	−5°C	−12°C
Harbin	−12°C	−24°C
Reykjavik	5°C	−3°C
Anchorage	−8°C	−16°C

   A Ottawa   **B** Moscow   **C** Harbin   **D** Reykjavik   **E** Anchorage

10   Florence went shopping for these ingredients.

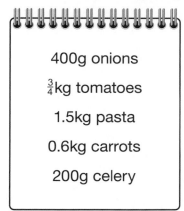

400g onions

$\frac{3}{4}$kg tomatoes

1.5kg pasta

0.6kg carrots

200g celery

What is the total weight of food that she had to carry home?

A 3.9kg   B 4.45kg   C 4.25kg   D 6.1kg   E 3.45kg

---

11   In a year group of 57 children, two-thirds of them like swimming.

How many children do NOT like swimming?

A 18   B 36   C 19   D 21   E 38

---

12   **If Lela saves £3.25 every week, how many weeks will it take her to save enough to buy trainers that cost £48?**

A 12   B 13   C 14   D 15   E 16

---

13   A parallelogram has been drawn inside a rectangle.

What is the area of the parallelogram?

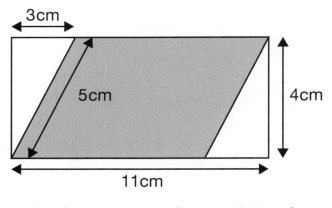

3cm

5cm

4cm

11cm

A 40cm²   B 55cm²   C 28cm²   D 44cm²   E 32cm²

14   The number 475,682 has been rounded to 476,000.

Which amount has it been rounded to?

A nearest 10,000

B nearest 100

C nearest 1000

D nearest 100,000

E nearest 10

15   The table shows estimates of the number of kilometres travelled by different birds in their lifetime.

Which bird travelled the shortest distance?

	Bird	Distance travelled (km)
A	Adelie penguin	352,000
B	Red knot	One hundred and forty-five thousand
C	Arctic tern	Two and a half million
D	Short-tailed shearwater	750,000
E	Bar-tailed godwit	Two hundred and fifty thousand

A Adelie   B Red   C Arctic   D Short-tailed   E Bar-tailed
   penguin   knot   tern   shearwater   godwit

16   Priya gets 34 out of 40 in a test.

What is that as a percentage?

A 84%   B 85%   C 86%   D 83%   E 82%

17   A team of four people run a cross-country relay race.

Each person runs a different distance: 6.1km, 3.7km, 5km and 4.6km.

How far do the team run altogether?

A 19.4km   B 32km   C 20km   D 20.4km   E 18.4km

18   The bar chart shows how many goals the school hockey team scored in each game this season.

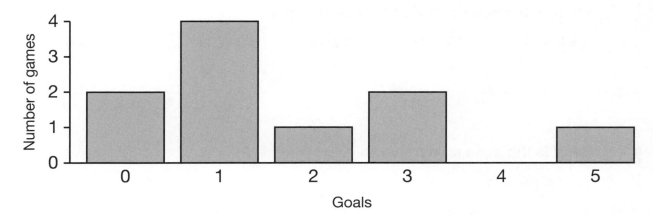

How many goals did they score overall?

A 18   B 11   C 16   D 17   E 10

19   Olivia thinks of a number. She subtracts 5 and halves it. She then adds 7 and gets the answer 16.

What was Olivia's starting number?

A 44   B 51   C 13   D 19   E 23

20   The area of a rectangle is 36cm².

What could NOT be the perimeter of the rectangle?

A 20cm   B 40cm   C 74cm   D 30cm   E 26cm

21   **Which number completes this calculation?**

$$\frac{?}{12} + \frac{1}{?} = \frac{7}{12}$$

A 2   B 6   C 1   D 3   E 5

22   Eddie begins a 105km journey at 8.20am. He travels at an average speed of 60km per hour.

What time does he arrive at his destination?

A 9.05am   B 10.20am   C 10.05am   D 9.20am   E 10.50am

---

23   **What is the missing number?**

$1.5 \times 6 = ? \div (5 \times 1.4)$

A 56   B 72   C 2   D 48   E 63

---

24   The diagram shows a shape drawn on a coordinate grid.

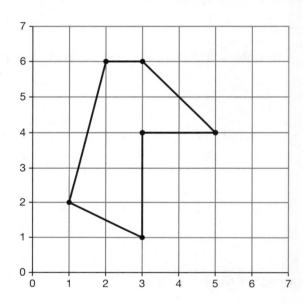

Which coordinate is at the vertex of a 45° angle?

A (1, 2)   B (3, 1)   C (3, 4)   D (5, 4)   E (6, 2)

---

25   **A triangular prism has how many triangular faces?**

A 1   B 2   C 3   D 4   E 5

Non-verbal Reasoning

Codes

On the left are some shapes and their codes. You must find out what each code letter represents. Then find the correct code for the last shape from the set of five codes on the right. Mark your answers on the answer sheet on page 36.

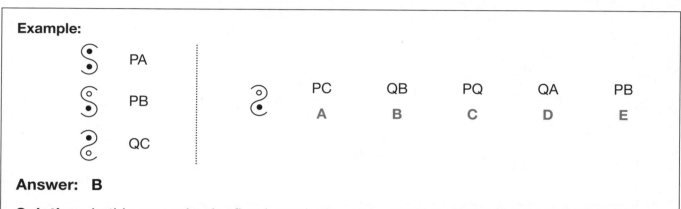

Example:

	PA
	PB
	QC

PC   QB   PQ   QA   PB
A   B   C   D   E

Answer: B

Solution: In this example, the first letter is the same for both S shapes, so P is the code for the S shape and Q is the code for the reverse S shape. The second letter is different for each shape, so A, B and C must be the codes for the black and white dot arrangements. So the answer is QB and **B** has been marked on the answer sheet.

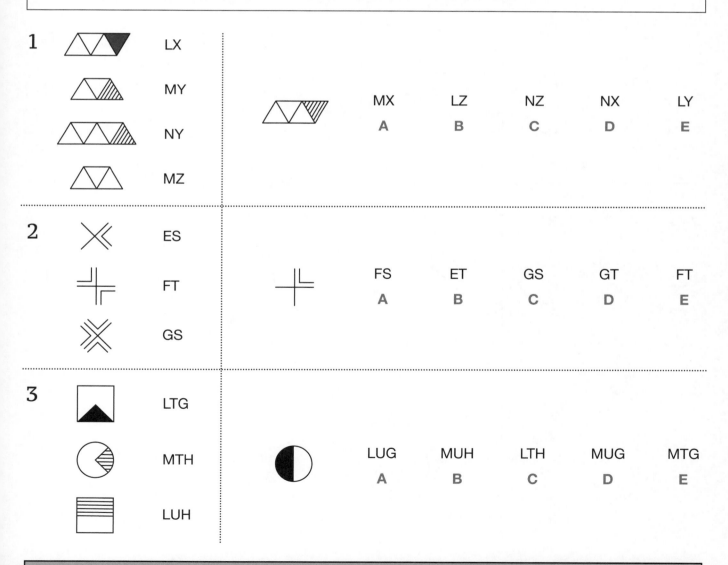

1

	LX
	MY
	NY
	MZ

MX   LZ   NZ   NX   LY
A   B   C   D   E

2

	ES
	FT
	GS

FS   ET   GS   GT   FT
A   B   C   D   E

3

	LTG
	MTH
	LUH

LUG   MUH   LTH   MUG   MTG
A   B   C   D   E

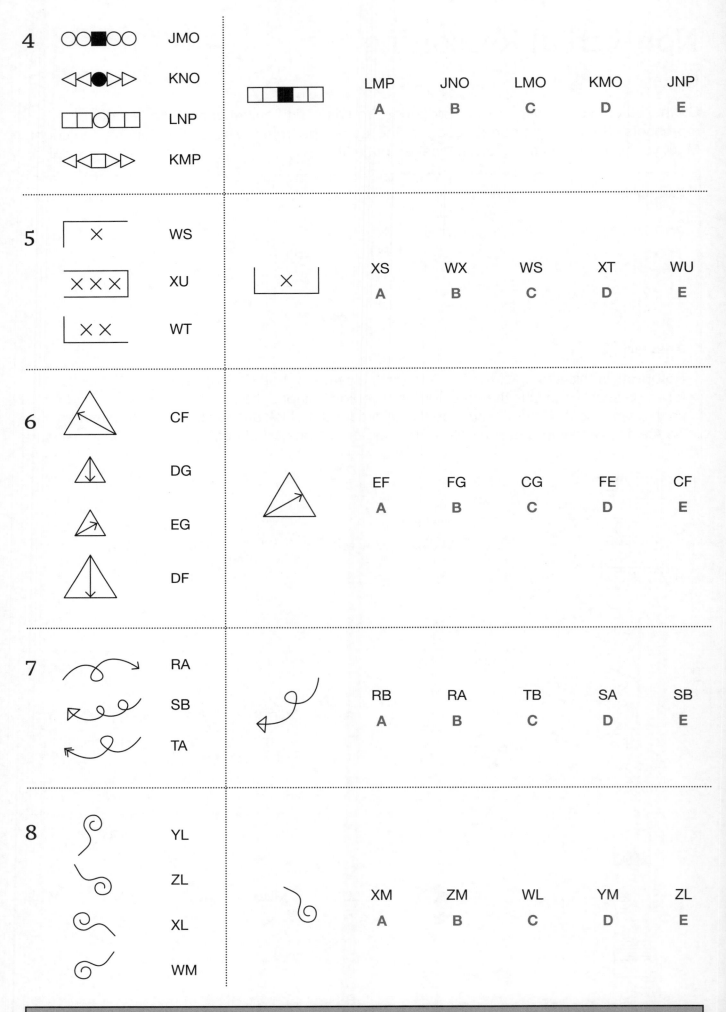

4

○○■○○ JMO

◁◁●▷▷ KNO

☐☐○☐☐ LNP

◁◁☐▷▷ KMP

	LMP	JNO	LMO	KMO	JNP
	A	**B**	**C**	**D**	**E**

5

WS

XU

WT

	XS	WX	WS	XT	WU
	A	**B**	**C**	**D**	**E**

6

CF

DG

EG

DF

	EF	FG	CG	FE	CF
	A	**B**	**C**	**D**	**E**

7

RA

SB

TA

	RB	RA	TB	SA	SB
	A	**B**	**C**	**D**	**E**

8

YL

ZL

XL

WM

	XM	ZM	WL	YM	ZL
	A	**B**	**C**	**D**	**E**

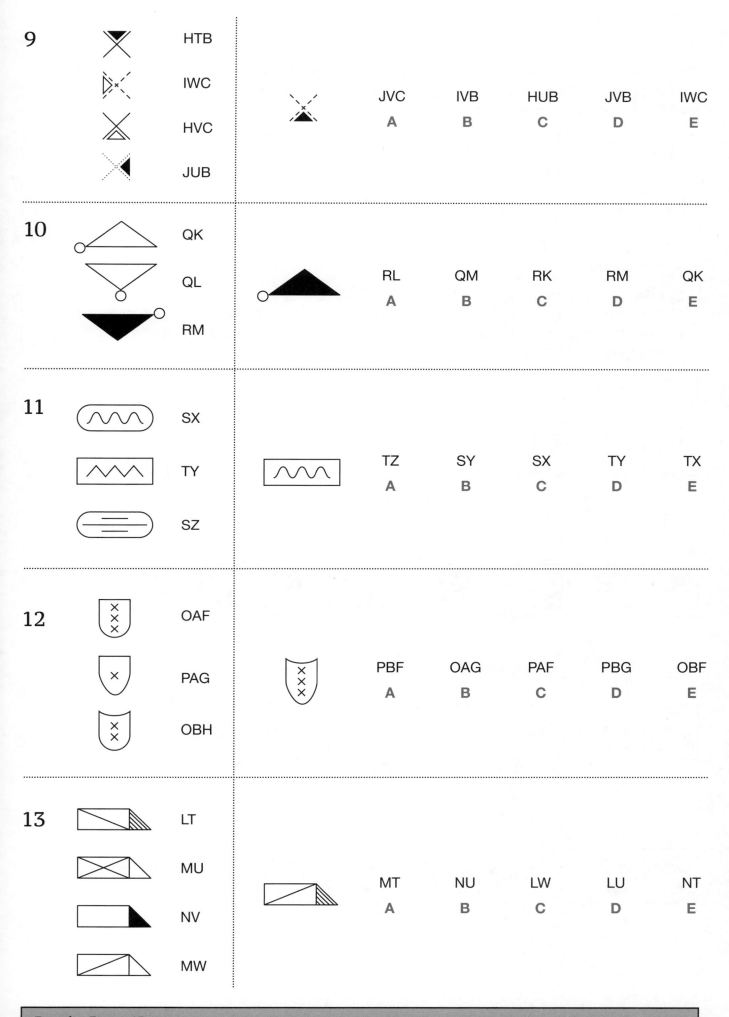

9

HTB

IWC

HVC

JUB

	JVC	IVB	HUB	JVB	IWC
	A	**B**	**C**	**D**	**E**

10

QK

QL

RM

	RL	QM	RK	RM	QK
	A	**B**	**C**	**D**	**E**

11

SX

TY

SZ

	TZ	SY	SX	TY	TX
	A	**B**	**C**	**D**	**E**

12

OAF

PAG

OBH

	PBF	OAG	PAF	PBG	OBF
	A	**B**	**C**	**D**	**E**

13

LT

MU

NV

MW

	MT	NU	LW	LU	NT
	A	**B**	**C**	**D**	**E**

Series

There are five squares arranged in order with one square left empty. One of the five squares on the right **replaces** the empty square on the left to complete the sequence. Mark your answers on the answer sheet on page 36.

Example:

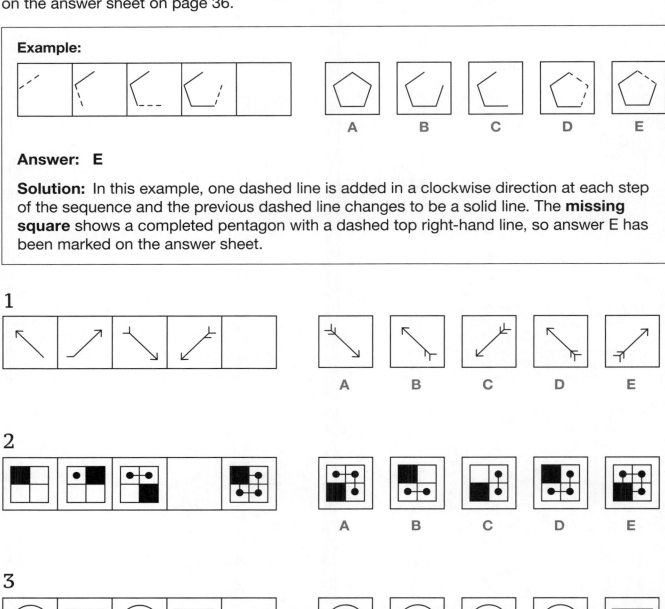

Answer: E

Solution: In this example, one dashed line is added in a clockwise direction at each step of the sequence and the previous dashed line changes to be a solid line. The **missing square** shows a completed pentagon with a dashed top right-hand line, so answer E has been marked on the answer sheet.

1

2

3

4

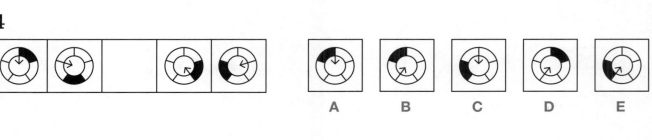

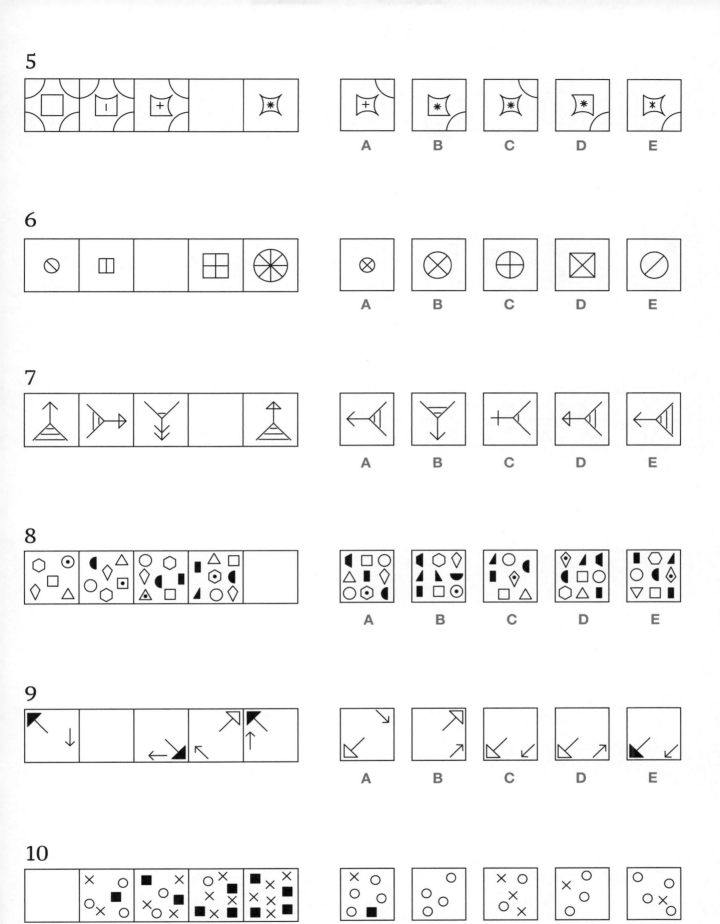

11

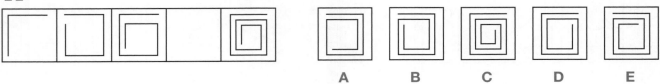

A   B   C   D   E

12

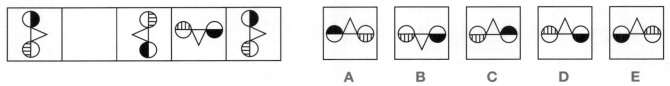

A   B   C   D   E

13

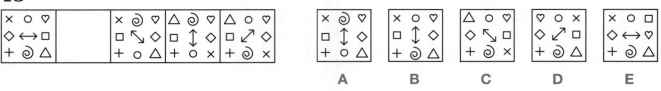

A   B   C   D   E

11+ Practice Paper 2A English and Verbal Reasoning

Information about this practice paper:

1. This paper is multiple choice. Mark your answer to each question in pencil on the answer sheet. Draw a firm line clearly through the rectangle on the answer sheet. If you make a mistake, rub it out and write in your new answer.

2. For pages 32 and 41–42, you have to read a text and then answer some questions about it. You can go back to the text to check your answers as many times as you want. There are also some spelling, punctuation and grammar exercises to do on pages 43–45.

3. Pages 46–51 have different types of questions. Each question starts with an explanation of what to do, followed by an example and solution with the answer marked on the answer sheet.

4. Some questions require more than one answer to be marked. Read the instructions carefully.

5. You may find some of the questions difficult. If you get stuck, **go to the next question**. If you are not sure, choose the answer you think is best.

6. Work as quickly and as carefully as you can.

 You have 50 minutes to complete this paper.

English

Read the text and then answer the questions that follow on pages 41–42.

Roman Writers

1. Introduction

Writing was very important in Ancient Rome. From the evidence of letters, public records, graffiti, inscriptions on pottery and mosaics, it is clear that quite a few Romans learned to read and write. The most famous writers were treated as major celebrities and supported by emperors and wealthy Romans. Although many of their books and letters have been lost over the years, enough have survived for us to
5 see why many of these writers were popular in Roman times.

2. The Poet – Virgil (70–19BC)

It is believed that Virgil was born and brought up in a small village in northern Italy. His early poetry was inspired by his observations of the farmers and peasants who worked tirelessly on the land. It was the first time poems were written about ordinary Roman people instead of gods and famous heroes.

In the last ten years of his life, Virgil wrote his epic poem, *The Aeneid*, which retells the dramatic stories
10 about the fall of Troy and how Rome was founded. While he was dying, Virgil horrified his many followers when he requested that the whole poem was to be burned after his death. Luckily, Emperor Augustus intervened and *The Aeneid* was saved for generations to read and enjoy.

3. The Playwright – Plautus (*c*.254–184BC)

Plays were very popular. Most were based on Ancient Greek stories then adapted for a Roman audience. They were usually performed in the daytime in public areas, such as a theatre or arena.

15 One of the most celebrated Roman playwrights was Plautus, who was known for his hilarious slapstick comedies full of puns, metaphors and jokes.

Here is a line from one of Plautus's plays.

'My father is a fly: you can't keep anything secret from him; he's always buzzing around.'

People would come in droves to enjoy the dancing, singing and topsy-turvy spectacles. They were like
20 today's pantomimes.

4. The Letter Writer – Pliny the Younger (*c*.AD61–112)

Pliny the Younger wrote lots of speeches and poetry, but he was particularly famous for his books of letters which commented on the good and bad aspects of Roman life.

When he was 18, Pliny the Younger wrote a memorable eyewitness account of the volcanic eruption of Mount Vesuvius in AD79. During that time, Pliny was living with his uncle, Pliny the Elder, in
25 Pompeii. Unlike his uncle, he survived the eruption and wrote some of his account looking back at Pompeii from his rescue ship. In one vivid description, he notes how the thick volcanic smoke seemed to erupt upwards into the shape of a pine tree with its tall trunk and spreading branches.

In another part of his letters, Pliny offers an interesting insight into the remarkable character of his uncle. To help calm a friend's fears, Pliny the Elder demonstrated that all would be fine by continuing
30 with his regular bath and dinner while the volcano was erupting. Pliny the Younger notes that his uncle successfully gave the impression of being cheerful, although secretly he may have been pretending, which in Pliny the Younger's opinion was just as brave.

We can gain a valuable insight into the lives of Ancient Romans thanks to the survival of some the inspirational works written by these famous Roman writers.

Answer sheets

Practice Paper 1A: English and Verbal Reasoning
Student name:

Please mark the boxes with a horizontal line like this ▭.

English: The Dragon's Pearl (pages 6–8)

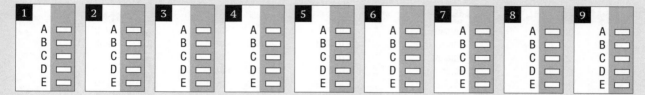

Anni's Rainforest (page 9)

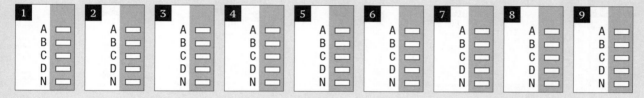

Dear Diary (page 10)

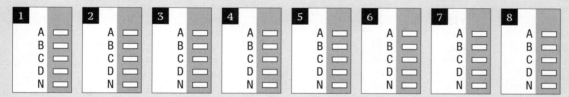

Night Terror (page 11)

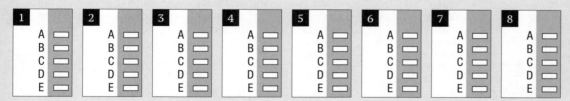

Verbal Reasoning (page 12)

Answer sheets

Practice Paper 1A: English and Verbal Reasoning

Student name:

Please mark the boxes with a horizontal line like this ▭.

Verbal Reasoning (page 13)

Example	1	2	3	4	5
tall ▭	grass ▭	rocket ▭	time ▭	shirt ▭	swim ▭
happy ▭	wet ▭	hero ▭	month ▭	hat ▭	walk ▭
green ▭	arid ▭	planet ▭	day ▭	belt ▭	fast ▭
table ▭	dry ▭	star ▭	heavy ▭	scarf ▭	run ▭
red ▭	hot ▭	hot ▭	length ▭	shoes ▭	slow ▭
high ▭	sand ▭	holiday ▭	shape ▭	collar ▭	kick ▭

(page 14)

Example	1	2	3	4	5
OQ ▭	GT ▭	EG ▭	XZ ▭	QP ▭	TP ▭
OP ▭	CX ▭	MO ▭	WY ▭	UW ▭	KM ▭
KL ▭	BY ▭	QS ▭	UY ▭	RP ▭	TR ▭
PQ ▭	HS ▭	QT ▭	VT ▭	SP ▭	TW ▭
NO ▭	AZ ▭	OP ▭	US ▭	XY ▭	RN ▭

(page 15)

Example	1	2	3	4	5
hot ▭	red ▭	hand ▭	rang ▭	cramp ▭	mess ▭
ten ▭	mend ▭	lash ▭	sing ▭	cream ▭	nice ▭
top ▭	rub ▭	wind ▭	wing ▭	clamp ▭	mass ▭
pen ▭	bed ▭	wish ▭	sung ▭	crepe ▭	mice ▭
hen ▭	dub ▭	wand ▭	ring ▭	creep ▭	acre ▭

(page 16)

Example	1	2	3	4
cook ▭	reply ▭	dangerous ▭	spectator ▭	solid ▭
mix ▭	share ▭	energy ▭	athlete ▭	flexible ▭
divide ▭	explain ▭	delicate ▭	driver ▭	difficult ▭
blend ▭	letter ▭	fragile ▭	instructor ▭	bendy ▭
paint ▭	answer ▭	strong ▭	singer ▭	round ▭
friendly ▭	ask ▭	safe ▭	observer ▭	liquid ▭

(page 17)

Example	1	2	3	4	5
10 ▭	21 ▭	14 ▭	100 ▭	17 ▭	30 ▭
11 ▭	20 ▭	8 ▭	94 ▭	19 ▭	21 ▭
13 ▭	19 ▭	16 ▭	110 ▭	20 ▭	22 ▭
18 ▭	22 ▭	4 ▭	117 ▭	21 ▭	28 ▭
16 ▭	30 ▭	13 ▭	84 ▭	16 ▭	34 ▭

Reading Question (page 17)

1
A ▭
B ▭
C ▭
D ▭

Answer sheets

Practice Paper 1B: Mathematics and Non-verbal Reasoning
Student name:

Please mark the boxes with a horizontal line like this ⊐.

Mathematics (pages 19–24)

1
- 41,367
- 430,607
- 413,600.7
- 413,670
- 413,607

2
- 140ml
- 320ml
- 120ml
- 240ml
- 540ml

3
- 47,256 > 47,265
- 63,629 < 62,693
- 24,214 > 24,124
- 82,502 < 80,255
- 19,347 < 18,437

4
- end in 3.
- be odd.
- be a multiple of 3.
- end in 5.
- be even.

5
- 18
- 22
- 36
- 42
- 72

6
- 4
- 5
- 6
- 7
- 8

7
- 2007
- 212
- 2120
- 2012
- 2002

8
- −185
- 12
- −147
- −427
- −72

9
- Ottawa
- Moscow
- Harbin
- Reykjavik
- Anchorage

10
- 3.9kg
- 4.45kg
- 4.25kg
- 6.1kg
- 3.45kg

11
- 18
- 36
- 19
- 21
- 38

12
- 12
- 13
- 14
- 15
- 16

13
- 40cm^2
- 55cm^2
- 28cm^2
- 44cm^2
- 32cm^2

14
- nearest 10,000
- nearest 100
- nearest 1000
- nearest 100,000
- nearest 10

15
- Adelie penguin
- Red knot
- Arctic tern
- Short-tailed shearwater
- Bar-tailed godwit

16
- 84%
- 85%
- 86%
- 83%
- 82%

17
- 19.4km
- 32km
- 20km
- 20.4km
- 18.4km

18
- 18
- 11
- 16
- 17
- 10

19
- 44
- 51
- 13
- 19
- 23

20
- 20cm
- 40cm
- 74cm
- 30cm
- 26cm

21
- 2
- 6
- 1
- 3
- 5

22
- 9.05am
- 10.20am
- 10.05am
- 9.20am
- 10.50am

23
- 56
- 72
- 2
- 48
- 63

24
- (1, 2)
- (3, 1)
- (3, 4)
- (5, 4)
- (6, 2)

25
- 1
- 2
- 3
- 4
- 5

Answer sheets

Practice Paper 1B: Mathematics and Non-verbal Reasoning

Student name:

Please mark the boxes with a horizontal line like this ▭.

Non-verbal Reasoning: **Codes** (pages 25–27)

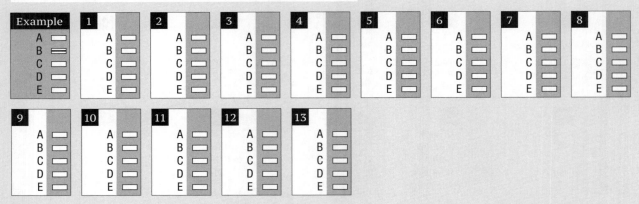

Series (pages 28–30)

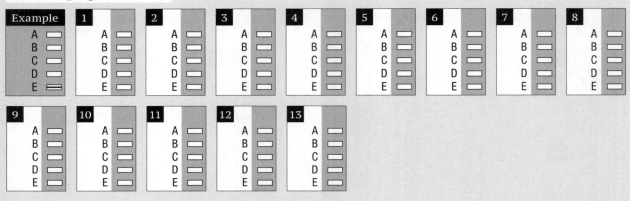

Answer sheets

Practice Paper 2A: English and Verbal Reasoning
Student name:

Please mark the boxes with a horizontal line like this ▭.

English: Roman Writers (pages 32 and 41–42)

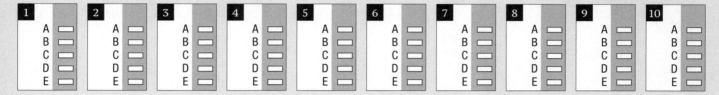

Punctuation (page 43)

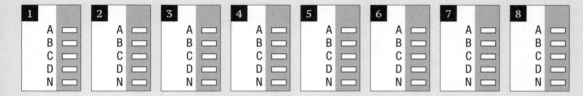

Spelling (page 44)

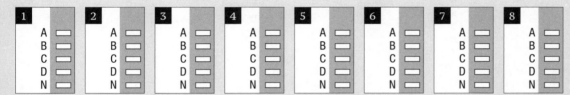

Grammar (page 45)

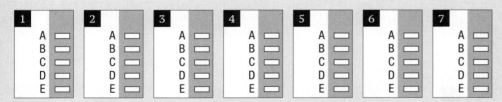

Answer sheets

Practice Paper 2A: English and Verbal Reasoning
Student name:

Please mark the boxes with a horizontal line like this ▬.

Verbal Reasoning (page 46)

Example	1	2	3	4	5
RED	TAN	EAT	SAT	BID	DAY
EAR	TOO	OAT	SON	BED	BEE
RAN	OUT	URN	SIT	TEN	TEA
ILL	PAN	OWL	SUN	WED	MEN
EYE	PIE	ALL	ZIP	SEA	KEY

(page 47)

Example	1	2	3	4	5
EQ	OL	ZA	SR	UT	HJ
BR	ON	YB	KL	TR	HM
ER	OP	YD	QR	QR	HI
ES	OM	XB	HI	UR	HG
EP	OR	ZB	PN	TV	HF

(page 48)

Example	1	2	3	4	5
p	s	s	q	r	s
l	p	n	u	a	h
a	o	a	i	n	e
n	r	c	t	g	l
k	t	k	e	e	l

(page 49)

Example	1	2	3	4	5
level	idea	destitute	aware	break	motivation
zigzag	plot	bad	announcement	smash	control
certificate	field	poor	detect	rest	drive
first	scheme	poverty	information	splinter	compel
unequal	acreage	shoddy	notice	pause	handle

(page 50)

Example	1	2	3	4	5
m	m	f	c	t	y
l	p	f	r	y	i
t	b	t	f	h	s
d	d	d	n	b	m
r	g	p	m	w	b
		l			

(page 51)

Example	1	2	3
4	11	2	10
2	12	4	8
3	13	3	5
5	10	5	4
1	20	1	3

Reading Question (page 51)

1
A
B
C
D
E

Answer sheets

Practice Paper 2B: Mathematics and Non-verbal Reasoning

Student name:

Please mark the boxes with a horizontal line like this ▭.

Mathematics (pages 53–58)

1
- 81
- 90
- 98
- 105
- 118

2
- $3\frac{3}{4}$
- $5\frac{1}{2}$
- $5\frac{1}{4}$
- $4\frac{1}{2}$
- 6

3
- 2868
- 2688
- 2588
- 2669
- 2698

4
- 4
- 5
- 10
- 8
- 6

5
- 6.5
- 6.7
- 6.57
- 6.4
- 6.47

6
- £2, £2, 50p, 20p, 5p, 1p
- £2, £1, 50p, 10p, 5p, 1p
- £2, £1, 20p, 20p, 10p
- £2, £2, 20p, 2p, 2p
- £5, 50p, 20p, 5p, 1p

7
- A
- B
- C
- D
- E

8
- 19
- 15
- 16
- 21
- 17

9
- 11
- 9
- 12
- 8
- 7

10
- 17°C
- 9°C
- −17°C
- −11°C
- −9°C

11
- 100°
- 125°
- 55°
- 119°
- 116°

12
- £254
- £248
- £238
- £224
- £242

13
- 18
- 9
- 21
- 14
- 6

14
- 7
- 4
- 5
- 3
- 6

15
- 22m
- 26m
- 31m
- 18m
- 28m

16
- 50 minutes
- 25 minutes
- 20 minutes
- 5 minutes
- 2.5 minutes

17
- 2.63 + 2.47
- 0.28 + 4.82
- 3.06 + 2.94
- 2.56 + 2.44
- 1.30 + 3.07

18
- 144cm³
- 48cm²
- 24cm²
- 144cm²
- 48cm³

19
- 80m
- −50m
- 60m
- 40m
- 70m

20
- 9
- 6
- 12
- 8
- 3

21
- 1 hour 45 minutes
- 141 minutes
- 101 minutes
- 1 hour 21 minutes
- 91 minutes

22
- (2, 0)
- (7, 5)
- (3, 1)
- (5, 2)
- (6, 4)

23
- 58
- 62
- 54
- 66
- 60

24
- 54
- 40
- 45
- 52
- 50

25
- A
- B
- C
- D
- E

Answer sheets

Practice Paper 2B: Mathematics and Non-verbal Reasoning

Student name:

Please mark the boxes with a horizontal line like this ▭.

Non-verbal Reasoning: Like Figures (pages 59–61)

Example	1	2	3	4	5	6	7	8
A ▭	A ▭	A ▭	A ▭	A ▭	A ▭	A ▭	A ▭	A ▭
B ▬	B ▭	B ▭	B ▭	B ▭	B ▭	B ▭	B ▭	B ▭
C ▭	C ▭	C ▭	C ▭	C ▭	C ▭	C ▭	C ▭	C ▭
D ▭	D ▭	D ▭	D ▭	D ▭	D ▭	D ▭	D ▭	D ▭
E ▭	E ▭	E ▭	E ▭	E ▭	E ▭	E ▭	E ▭	E ▭

9	10	11	12	13
A ▭	A ▭	A ▭	A ▭	A ▭
B ▭	B ▭	B ▭	B ▭	B ▭
C ▭	C ▭	C ▭	C ▭	C ▭
D ▭	D ▭	D ▭	D ▭	D ▭
E ▭	E ▭	E ▭	E ▭	E ▭

Analogies (pages 62–64)

Example	1	2	3	4	5	6	7	8
A ▭	A ▭	A ▭	A ▭	A ▭	A ▭	A ▭	A ▭	A ▭
B ▭	B ▭	B ▭	B ▭	B ▭	B ▭	B ▭	B ▭	B ▭
C ▭	C ▭	C ▭	C ▭	C ▭	C ▭	C ▭	C ▭	C ▭
D ▬	D ▭	D ▭	D ▭	D ▭	D ▭	D ▭	D ▭	D ▭
E ▭	E ▭	E ▭	E ▭	E ▭	E ▭	E ▭	E ▭	E ▭

9	10	11	12	13
A ▭	A ▭	A ▭	A ▭	A ▭
B ▭	B ▭	B ▭	B ▭	B ▭
C ▭	C ▭	C ▭	C ▭	C ▭
D ▭	D ▭	D ▭	D ▭	D ▭
E ▭	E ▭	E ▭	E ▭	E ▭

Answer the questions about the text on page 32. Mark your answers on the answer sheet on page 37.

1   **What is the main purpose of part 1?**

A   To introduce Roman writing and writers

B   To find out about Roman Britain

C   To learn about a famous Roman speech-writer

D   To learn about the Roman language

E   To find out who published Roman books

2   **Where did Virgil get his inspiration for his early poems?**

A   From conversations in town marketplaces

B   From folk stories and mosaics

C   From the farmers and peasants where he lived

D   From his family and friends

E   From the city of Rome

3   **Which statement about Virgil is NOT true?**

A   He was born in 70BC.

B   It took him many years to write *The Aeneid*.

C   He was born in northern Italy.

D   He wanted his poem to be published after he had died.

E   *The Aeneid* retold the story about the fall of Troy.

4   ***'My father is a fly: you can't keep anything secret from him; he's always buzzing around.'* (line 18)**

What is this line from a play by Plautus?

A   a pun

B   a metaphor

C   a joke

D   a simile

E   a rhyme

5   **About which event did Pliny the Younger write an eyewitness account in AD79?**

A   a battle with the Greeks

B   a massive earthquake

C   an exciting chariot race

D   the eruption of Mount Vesuvius

E   a speech read by Pliny the Elder to the Roman Emperor

6 **Why do you think Pliny the Younger thought his uncle was brave?**

   A   He went to search for a rescue ship.

   B   He wasn't afraid of the volcano eruption.

   C   He liked his bath water to be very hot.

   D   He planned a hike up to the volcano.

   E   He hid his fear to help his friend.

Answer these questions about the meaning of words in the text on page 32. Mark your answers on the answer sheet on page 37.

7 **Which word is closest in meaning to 'droves'? (line 19)**

   A   masses

   B   herds

   C   pairs

   D   vehicles

   E   a few

8 **Which word is closest in meaning to 'insight'? (line 28)**

   A   unawareness

   B   understanding

   C   entertainment

   D   education

   E   inability

Answer these questions about words and phrases as they are used in the text on page 32. Mark your answers on the answer sheet on page 37.

9 **What type of words are these?**

   Roman   **Italy**   *The Aeneid*   **Mount Vesuvius**   **Pliny the Elder**

   A   adjectives

   B   common nouns

   C   pronouns

   D   adverbs

   E   proper nouns

10 **'Luckily, Emperor Augustus intervened and *The Aeneid* was saved for generations to read and enjoy.' (lines 11–12)**

   How many adverbs are in this sentence?

   A   one   **D**   four

   B   two   **E**   five

   C   three

Punctuation

These sentences have some punctuation or capital letter mistakes. On each numbered line there is either one mistake or no mistake. Find the group of words containing the mistake and mark the letter of the group on the answer sheet. If there is no mistake, then select 'N'. Mark your answers on the answer sheet on page 37.

1   Today's tour of the Victorian sewers is cancelled the guide is unwell.
    A   B   C   D

2   As dawn broke, Gaskin Castle prepared itself for its enemy's inevitable attack.
    A   B   C   D

3   Thea leaped into the air. "We've won the national championship" she screamed.
    A   B   C   D

4   I can't wait to start growing parsnips, potatoes leeks and carrots on my new allotment.
    A   B   C   D

5   Rebecca discovered a small packet of chocolate covered raisins in her lunch box.
    A   B   C   D

6   How long does it take to sail to the Shetland islands from Aberdeen?
    A   B   C   D

7   "Run for your lives!" shouted Khalid. The volcano is on the verge of erupting."
    A   B   C   D

8   Dont swim into the caves! They can be dangerous places during high tide.
    A   B   C   D

Spelling

These sentences have some spelling mistakes. On each numbered line there is either one spelling mistake or no spelling mistake. Find the group of words containing the mistake and mark the letter of the group on the answer sheet. If there is no mistake, then select 'N'. Mark your answers on the answer sheet on page 37.

1 I could happyly spend all afternoon creating shapes out of the clouds.
      A   B   C   D

2 We wrote a class play based on the Greek mith about Pandora's box.
      A   B   C   D

3 The local town commitee have decided to organise a special winter fair.
      A   B   C   D

4 Bicycles are fine, but I prefer my gran's old three-wheeled tricycle.
      A   B   C   D

5 A dessert fox has large ears to help it cool down in the searing heat.
      A   B   C   D

6 To avoid being seen, Liam dragged himself across the floor on his stomack.
      A   B   C   D

7 Rosie nervously checked the clock; she was still only forth in the queue!
      A   B   C   D

8 My favourite food is called rösti. It's made from lots of grated potatos.
      A   B   C   D

Grammar

Choose a word or group of words to complete the sentences so that they make sense and use correct English. Mark the letter underneath your chosen word on the answer sheet on page 37.

1   If it had been sunny, we should of / would have / must of / did ought to have / will have
                                   A   B   C   D   E

    gone to the beach.

2   Queen Dhanya saddled up his / my / her / your / their beloved stallion.
                                      A   B   C   D   E

3   Leo was determined to be the best / bestest / most best / betterer / gooder table-tennis
                                      A   B   C   D   E

    player in the room.

4   The recycling bin are taken / is taken / are took / is took / is taking away
                              A   B   C   D   E

    every Monday.

5   We chose the funnier / more fun / funny / funniest / most funnier card in the shop.
                      A   B   C   D   E

6   We noticed a / these / them / lots / an unusual insect near the school pond.
                       A   B   C   D E

7   Zoe baked some fruit muffins when / after / before / as / because she went to bed.
                                    A   B   C   D   E

Verbal Reasoning

In sentences 1–5, the word in capitals has had **three letters** taken out. These letters can make one correctly spelled three-letter word.

The sentence must make sense. Mark your answers on the answer sheet on page 38.

Example:	Milo **HD** loud footsteps behind him.				
	A RED	B EAR	C RAN	D ILL	E EYE

Answer: **EAR**

Solution: The word in capitals is **HEARD**. The other three letter options do not make words.

1 The climber **SD** on top of the mountain peak.

   A TAN   B TOO   C OUT   D PAN   E PIE

2 My dog often **GRS** at my friend's cat.

   A EAT   B OAT   C URN   D OWL   E ALL

3 The Duke's ancient castle is now open to **VIORS**.

   A SAT   B SON   C SIT   D SUN   E ZIP

4 The servant girl was expected to be **OIENT**.

   A BID   B BED   C TEN   D WED   E SEA

5 Watch out for that **HOC** stick!

   A DAY   B BEE   C TEA   D MEN   E KEY

Find the next two letters in the series. Use the alphabet below to help you.

A B C D E F G H I J K L M N O P Q R S T U V W X Y Z

Mark your answers on the answer sheet on page 38.

Example: AS   BS   CR   DR   [?]

        A EQ   **B** BR   **C** ER   **D** ES   **E** EP

Answer: **EQ**

Solution: The first letters in each set are in alphabetical order. The second letters in each set match in pairs (AS – BS). After each pair, the second letter moves back one (SS – RR – QQ).

---

1   HK   KJ   JM   ML   LO   [?]

    A OL   **B** ON   **C** OP   **D** OM   **E** OR

2   UF   VE   WD   XC   [?]

    A ZA   **B** YB   **C** YD   **D** XB   **E** ZB

3   EF   VT   GH   SQ   IJ   [?]

    A SR   **B** KL   **C** QR   **D** HI   **E** PN

4   AB   ZY   CE   XV   FI   [?]

    A UT   **B** TR   **C** QR   **D** UR   **E** TV

5   CH   DF   EJ   FH   GL   [?]

    A HJ   **B** HM   **C** HI   **D** HG   **E** HF

In questions 1–5, make two new words by moving one letter from the first word to the second word.

Do not rearrange the letters in any other way and **both** the new words need to make sense. Mark your answers on the answer sheet on page 38.

Example:	plank		not		
	A p	**B** l	**C** a	**D** n	**E** k
Answer:	**k**				
Solution:	The two new words are **plan** and **knot**. Move the 'k' from 'plank'. Add it to the front of 'not' to make 'knot'.				

1 sport   yak

   A s   **B** p   **C** o   **D** r   **E** t

2 snack   tow

   A s   **B** n   **C** a   **D** c   **E** k

3 quite   rob

   A q   **B** u   **C** i   **D** t   **E** e

4 range   mad

   A r   **B** a   **C** n   **D** g   **E** e

5 shell   itch

   A s   **B** h   **C** e   **D** l   **E** l

In questions 1–5, there are two pairs of words.

Just **one** of the five given word answers will go well with **both** of the two pairs of words.

Find the word and mark your answers on the answer sheet on page 38.

Example: (even straight)   (position grade)

            A level   **B** zigzag   **C** certificate   **D** first   **E** unequal

Answer: **level**

Solution: The word **level** can describe whether something looks straight or even, such as a shelf. It can also describe what place or standard someone has achieved, eg 'Martha has reached the top level in maths'.

---

1   (plan conspire)   (land allotment)

        A idea   **B** plot   **C** field   **D** scheme   **E** acreage

2   (needy penniless)   (sub-standard dismal)

        A destitute   **B** bad   **C** poor   **D** poverty   **E** shoddy

3   (observe spot)   (poster advertisement)

        A aware   **B** announcement   **C** detect   **D** information   **E** notice

4   (crack shatter)   (interval playtime)

        A break   **B** smash   **C** rest   **D** splinter   **E** pause

5   (steer operate)   (determination ambition)

        A motivation   **B** control   **C** drive   **D** compel   **E** handle

In questions 1–5, the **same** letter must go into **both** sets of brackets. The letter ends the word in front of the brackets and begins the word after the brackets.

Mark your answers on the answer sheet on page 38.

Example: boa [?] usk   car [?] ime

A m   B l   C t   D d   E r

Answer: t

Solution: The four words are **boat**, **tusk**, **cart**, **time**. Only the letter 't' can be added at the end and beginning of the four words.

---

1   fla [?] ush   tra [?] ear

A m   B p   C b   D d   E g

2   gol [?] rop   hea [?] own

A f   B t   C d   D p   E l

3   basi [?] udge   wide [?] ote

A c   B r   C f   D n   E m

4   slo [?] ood   allo [?] and

A t   B y   C h   D b   E w

5   sk [?] ell   hand [?] ellow

A y   B i   C s   D m   E b

In questions 1–3, find the number that finishes the calculation.

Mark your answers on the answer sheet on page 38.

Example: $4 + 3 = 5 + [\,?\,]$

      A 4   **B** 2   **C** 3   **D** 5   **E** 1

Answer: **2**

Solution: $4 + 3 = 7$ $5 + 2 = 7$

---

1 $59 - 7 = 32 + [\,?\,]$

    A 11   **B** 12   **C** 13   **D** 10   **E** 20

2 $7 \times 3 + 12 = 10 \times 3 + [\,?\,]$

    A 2   **B** 4   **C** 3   **D** 5   **E** 1

3 $48 \div 8 \times 4 = 5 \times [\,?\,] + 4$

    A 10   **B** 8   **C** 5   **D** 4   **E** 3

Read the information below, then work out the answer to the question. Mark your answer on the answer sheet on page 38.

1   Jaden, Thea and Antoni are having swimming lessons.

    Thea has just got her 25m swimming certificate.

    Jaden has been able to swim 50m since last term.

    Only one of the sentences below **must** be true.

    Which one?

    A   Antoni has his 25m swimming certificate.

    B   Jaden is a stronger swimmer than Thea.

    C   Thea can sometimes swim 50m.

    D   Antoni can swim faster than Jaden.

    E   Jaden has just got his 50m swimming certificate.

11+ Practice Paper 2B Mathematics and Non-verbal Reasoning

Information about this practice paper:

1. This paper is multiple choice. Mark your answer to each question in pencil on the answer sheet beginning on page 39. Draw a firm line clearly through the rectangle on the answer sheet. If you make a mistake, rub it out and write in your new answer.

2. Pages 53–58 contain mathematics questions. Read all of the questions carefully.

3. Pages 59–64 contain two different picture-based question types. Each question starts with an explanation of what to do, followed by an example and the solution with the answer marked on the answer sheet.

4. You may find some of the questions difficult. If you get stuck, **go to the next question**. If you are not sure, choose the answer you think is best.

5. **Work as quickly and as carefully as you can.**

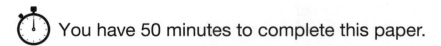 You have 50 minutes to complete this paper.

Mathematics

Mark your answers to the following questions on the answer sheet on page 39.

1   **Which number is in the wrong place?**

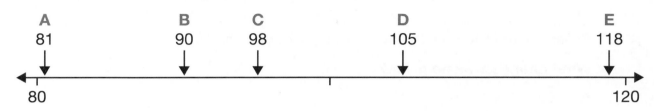

A	B	C	D	E
81	90	98	105	118

80   120

2   Look at this number machine.

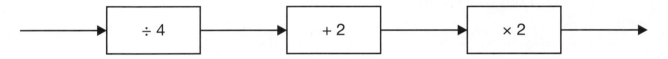

$\div 4$ $+ 2$ $\times 2$

If 3 goes in, what comes out?

A $3\frac{3}{4}$ B $5\frac{1}{2}$ C $5\frac{1}{4}$ D $4\frac{1}{2}$ E 6

3   A coach driver drives 842 miles one week, 1169 miles the next week and 677 miles the week after that.

How many miles did she drive altogether?

A 2868   B 2688   C 2588   D 2669   E 2698

4   The pictogram shows the number of bananas eaten by a class each day. They ate a total of 112 in the five days.

Monday	🍌🍌🍌
Tuesday	🍌🍌🍌
Wednesday	🍌🍌🍌🍌
Thursday	🍌🍌🍌
Friday	🍌🍌

How many bananas are represented by each banana symbol in the pictogram?

A 4   B 5   C 10   D 8   E 6

5   **Round this number to the nearest tenth.**

6.47

A 6.5   B 6.7   C 6.57   D 6.4   E 6.47

---

6   Safian used a £10 note to pay for some shopping that cost £6.34.

What change was he given?

A   £2, £2, 50p, 20p, 5p, 1p

B   £2, £1, 50p, 10p, 5p, 1p

C   £2, £1, 20p, 20p, 10p

D   £2, £2, 20p, 2p, 2p

E   £5, 50p, 20p, 5p, 1p

---

7   **Which of these nets will NOT make a cube?**

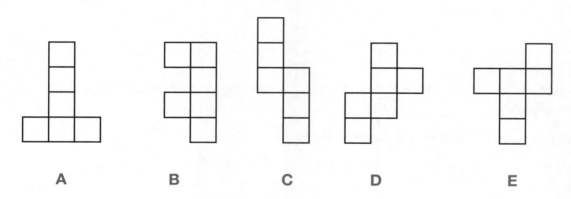

A   B   C   D   E

---

8   **Which number comes next in this sequence?**

| 2 | 3 | 5 | 7 | 11 | 13 |

A 19   B 15   C 16   D 21   E 17

---

9   Class 6L plant some strawberry plants. Slugs eat four of the plants and each of the rest of the plants grows nine strawberries.

If the children pick 63 strawberries, how many plants did they start with?

A 11   B 9   C 12   D 8   E 7

10 At midday the temperature was 4°C. By midnight the temperature had fallen by 13°C.

What was the temperature at midnight?

A 17°C   B 9°C   C −17°C   D −11°C   E −9°C

11

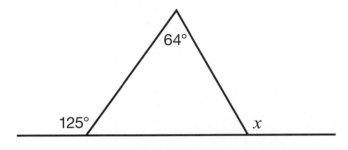

What is the size of angle x?

A 100°   B 125°   C 55°   D 119°   E 116°

---

12 A bike normally costs £280, but is reduced by 15% in a sale.

How much does it cost now?

A £254   B £248   C £238   D £224   E £242

---

13 **Which number is in the wrong section of the Venn diagram?**

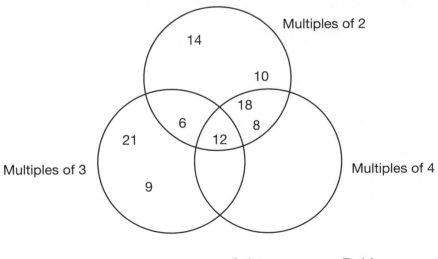

A 18   B 9   C 21   D 14   E 6

14 Emma started at 10 and counted backwards in steps of $1\frac{3}{4}$.

Which of these was in her sequence?

A 7   B 4   C 5   D 3   E 6

---

15 A swimming pool needs to be fenced off for safety with a gap of 1 metre between the edge of the pool and the fence. One side already has a wall and doesn't need to be fenced.

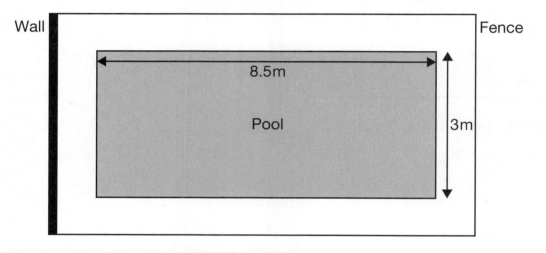

Wall   Pool   8.5m   3m   Fence

What length of fencing will be needed?

A 22m   B 26m   C 31m   D 18m   E 28m

---

16 Water is dripping from a pipe at a rate of 40ml every five minutes.

How long will it take for 0.2 litres of water to leak from the pipe?

A 50 minutes   B 25 minutes   C 20 minutes   D 5 minutes   E 2.5 minutes

---

17 **Which of these add up to 5?**

A   2.63 + 2.47

B   0.28 + 4.82

C   3.06 + 2.94

D   2.56 + 2.44

E   1.30 + 3.07

18 **What is the area of a square with a side measuring 12cm?**

A 144cm³   **B** 48cm²   **C** 24cm²   **D** 144cm²   **E** 48cm³

---

19 **What is the total height of this iceberg?**

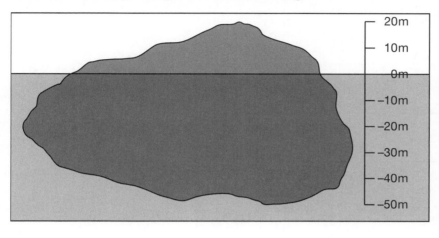

A 80m   **B** –50m   **C** 60m   **D** 40m   **E** 70m

---

20 **What is the highest common factor of 42 and 90?**

A 9   **B** 6   **C** 12   **D** 8   **E** 3

---

21 Here is part of a railway timetable.

London Euston	11:45	12:42	13:40	14:35
Crewe	13:15	14:09	15:11	16:08
Wilmslow	13:32	14:23	15:27	16:24
Manchester	13:50	14:39	15:46	16:43

How long is the 12:42 from London Euston expected to take to reach Wilmslow?

A   1 hour 45 minutes

B   141 minutes

C   101 minutes

D   1 hour 21 minutes

E   91 minutes

22 Four of these coordinates are the same distance from M as they are from N.

Which coordinate is not the same distance from M and N?

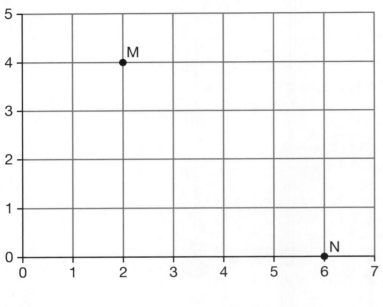

A (2, 0)　　　　B (7, 5)　　　　C (3, 1)　　　　D (5, 2)　　　　E (6, 4)

---

23 Children break up for summer at 3.15pm on Thursday 8 July. The first day of the summer holiday is Friday 9 July. The children go back to school on Monday 5 September.

How many days long is the holiday?

A 58　　　　B 62　　　　C 54　　　　D 66　　　　E 60

---

24 A farmer is packing eggs in boxes of 12.

How many boxes are needed for 540 eggs?

A 54　　　　B 40　　　　C 45　　　　D 52　　　　E 50

---

25 **Which shape has two pairs of parallel lines and one pair of perpendicular lines?**

A　　　　　　B　　　　　　C　　　　　　D　　　　　　E

Non-verbal Reasoning

Like Figures

On the left there are three figures that are **alike**. On the right, one of the five figures is **most like** the three figures on the left. Mark your answers on the answer sheet on page 40.

Example:

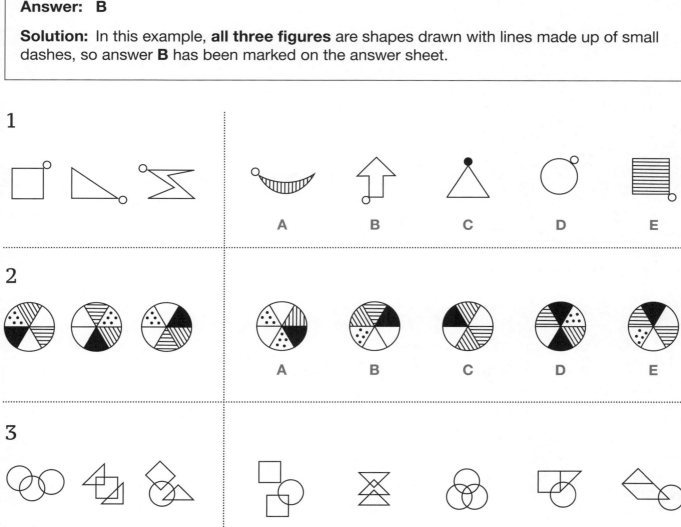

Answer: B

Solution: In this example, **all three figures** are shapes drawn with lines made up of small dashes, so answer **B** has been marked on the answer sheet.

1

2

3

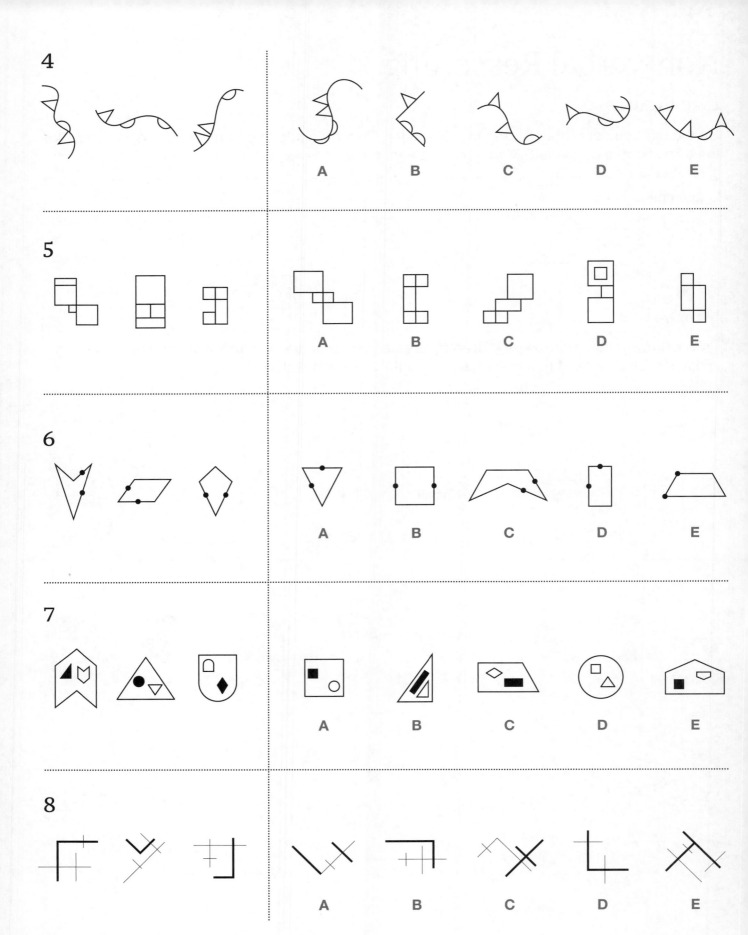

4

5

6

7

8

9

| A | B | C | D | E |

10

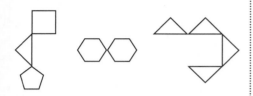 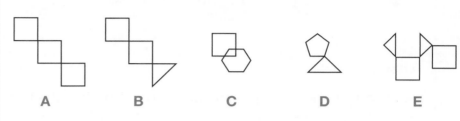

| A | B | C | D | E |

11

| A | B | C | D | E |

12

| A | B | C | D | E |

13

| A | B | C | D | E |

Analogies

On the left there are two shapes with an arrow between them. Decide what changes have been made to the shape on the left to create the shape on the right. Then look at the third shape, the arrow next to it and five more shapes. Decide which of the five shapes completes the second pair in the same way as the first pair. Mark your answers on the answer sheet on page 40.

Example:

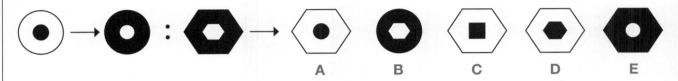

Answer: D

Solution: In this example, the **second shape** has the shading from the **first shape** reversed while the shapes remain the same. Black becomes white and white becomes black, so answer **D** has been marked on the answer sheet.

1

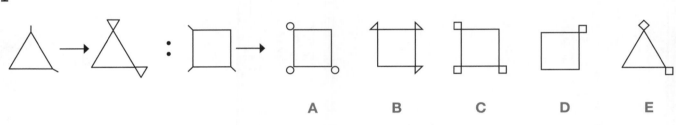

2

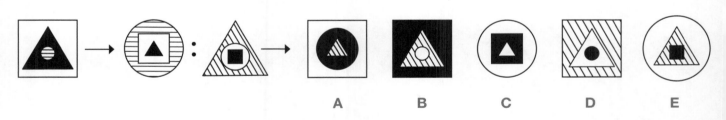

3

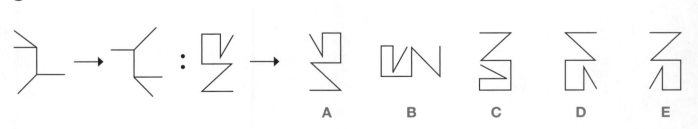

4

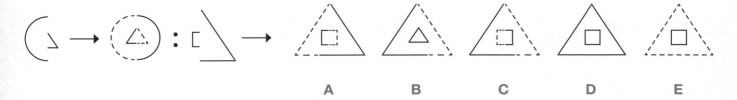

A B C D E

5

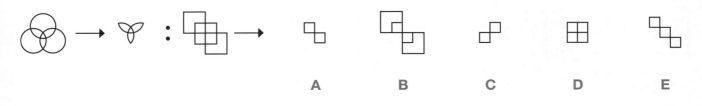

A B C D E

6

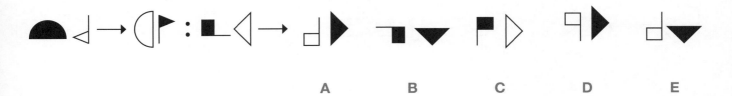

A B C D E

7

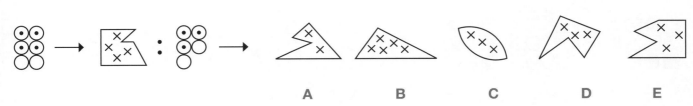

A B C D E

8

A B C D E

9

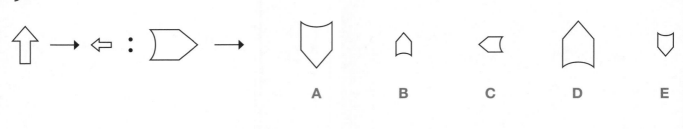

A   B   C   D   E

10

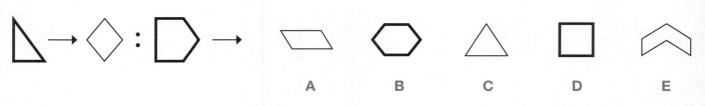

A   B   C   D   E

11

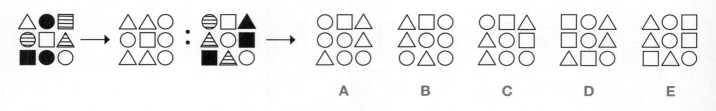

A   B   C   D   E

12

A   B   C   D   E

13

A   B   C   D   E

Answers

Practice Paper 1A: English and Verbal Reasoning

English: The Dragon's Pearl (pages 6–8)

1	B	The boy and his mother were close to starvation. The drought had caused the fields to dry up so not a lot of crops could be grown.
2	C	To find fresh green grass. The boy was running out of places he could go to find good grass.
3	A	Thoughtful. Examples in the text include him caring for his mother, using money to buy food for both of them and sharing his good luck with villagers.
4	E	The pearl increased things wherever it was placed. Examples include a patch of grass, rice and other foods.
5	D	The mother threw the pearl into a well. All the other actions and events are true when some villagers decided they wanted the pearl.
6	A	The simile in this phrase is 'like old friends greeting each other'. It gives the impression that the dry cracks were happy to be joined again into a healthier soil.
7	E	People believed that the river dragon went on to always protect their land from natural disasters. The thoughtful boy was now a protective, caring dragon.
8	B	The word 'tentatively' in line 9 has the same meaning as 'carefully'.
9	D	The word 'diminished' in line 2 is a verb. It means 'to shrink' or 'lessen'. The 'River Min gradually diminished into muddy puddles' means that the drought caused the water of the River Min to dry up and leave just 'muddy puddles'.

Anni's Rainforest (page 9)

1	C	A capital letter is needed for the proper noun '**A**nni's'.
2	N	No mistake
3	B	A capital letter is needed for '**H**e' to show the start of a sentence.
4	A	A possessive apostrophe is needed to indicate that Sinchi is in his cousin Anni's village: **cousin's village**.
5	D	A full stop is needed at the end of the speech sentence: "I want to find out why you like the forest so much."
6	B	A comma is needed after a fronted adverbial phrase: 'With a sigh of resignation, Anni…'. The comma separates the phrase from the main clause and shows a natural verbal pause.
7	C	A question mark is used incorrectly in this phrase, "What a dump?" It should be an exclamation mark: "What a dump**!**"
8	A	A comma is needed in a list of adjectives: "It's just a **noisy, smelly** wood!"
9	C	A contraction apostrophe is missing for the contraction 'would**n't**'.

Dear Diary (page 10)

1	D	**exception** The suffix 'ion' is often used if the root word ends in 't' or 'te', for example, 'except – exception'.
2	B	**fort** 'fort' means a small castle or army base. Its homophone word 'fought' is the past tense verb of 'fight'.
3	C	**legion** The letters 'gi' in 'legion' make the /j/ sound, as in 'giant'.
4	B	**patrol** There is only one 'l' at the end of the word 'patrol'.
5	N	**No mistake**
6	A	**steady** The word 'steady' uses 'ea' for the short vowel /e/ sound, as in 'head', 'bread'.
7	B	**believe** We use 'ie' when it has a long vowel /e/ sound, as in 'field', 'chief'.
8	B	**actually** 'actually' is an adverb. We add 'ly' straight onto most adjectives that end in a consonant 'actual -ly'.

Night Terror (page 11)

1	B	**sat** Use the past tense action verb for 'sit'. We use 'seated' for when we put someone into a seat.
2	D	**had woken** This sentence is in the past perfect tense. We use 'had' before the past participle for 'wake', which is 'woken'.
3	A	**was** The sentence is in the past tense. We use the 'being verb' – 'was' – to show a singular object.
4	C	**Despite** This word introduces or links the two contrasting images of Fred being 'cocooned in a warm bed' and he 'couldn't stop shivering.' in question 5.
5	E	**couldn't** The contracted word for 'could not', which means it was difficult or impossible to 'stop shivering'.
6	B	**across** This is a prepositional word. It is the only one that makes sense in the sentence.
7	D	**tried** The past tense verb for 'try'. For root verbs that end in '-y', we often replace the 'y' with an 'i' and then add '-ed'.
8	A	**his** This is a possessive pronoun. We use it before a noun to show what the main subject in a sentence owns. In the text, it is about a boy, so the correct pronoun would be '**his** mouth'.

Verbal Reasoning (page 12)

1	A	**Listen to** The hidden word is 'tent'. Lis**ten to** the patter of rain.
2	E	**yellow ink?** The hidden word is 'wink'. Have you got any yello**w ink**?
3	C	**grabbed gems** The hidden word is 'edge'. The thief grabb**ed ge**ms with diamonds.
4	B	**puffin dived** The hidden word is 'find'. The puf**fin d**ived off the cliff.

(page 13)

1	B, X	**wet; dry** An ocean is 'wet'. A desert is 'dry'.
2	C, X	**planet; star** Jupiter is described as a 'planet'. The Sun is described as a 'star'.
3	A, Y	**time; length** A minute is a measurement of 'time'. A metre is a measurement of 'length'.
4	A, Y	**shirt; shoes** Buttons can fasten up a 'shirt'. Laces can fasten up 'shoes'.
5	B, X	**walk; run** Stroll is another word for 'walk'. Sprint is another word for 'run'.

(page 14)

1	A	**GT** To get EV from DW, DW are the fourth letters in from left (A–D) and right (Z–W). EV are the fifth letters along from left and right. To follow the pattern, the next letters after FU (sixth) are GT.
2	C	**QS** To get GI from BD, count three letters from D to G; count two letters from G to get letter I. To follow the pattern for LN, count three letters from N to get Q; count two letters from Q to get S.
3	B	**WY** To get NP from MQ, N is the letter after M; P is the letter before Q. Follow the pattern to get WY from VZ – W comes after V and Y comes before Z.
4	A	**QP** To get BA from HD, count 6 letters back from H to get B. Count 3 letters back from D to get A. Follow the pattern for WS. Count back six letters from W to get to Q; count 3 letters back from S to get P.
5	A	**TP** To get KG from ML, count two letters back from M to get K; count four letters back from K to get G. Follow the pattern for VU. Count two letters back from V to get T. Count four letters back from T to get P.

(page 15)

1	C	**rub** – second and third letters from first word and first letter from second word. (s**ki**n [kid] **d**amp) (d**ru**m [rub] **b**end)
2	E	**wand** – first letter from first word and last three letters from second word. (**l**oan [list] m**ist**) (**w**ish [wand] l**and**)
3	A	**rang** – third and fourth letters from first word and the final two letters from second word. (ta**bl**e [blow] gr**ow**) (st**ra**w [rang] cli**ng**)
4	B	**cream** – first, second and third letters from first word and first and second letters from second word. (**cru**mb [crush] **sh**elf) (**cre**ak [cream] **am**ple)
5	D	**mice** – first and third letters from first word and first and third letters from second word. (**c**l**a**ss [cage] **g**r**e**en) (**m**a**i**n [mice] **c**r**e**ss)

(page 16)

1	A, Y	**reply; answer** Both words can mean a response to something being asked.
2	C, X	**delicate; fragile** Both words can mean something that is easily broken.
3	A, Z	**spectator; observer** Both words can mean someone who watches something.
4	B, X	**flexible; bendy** Both words can mean something or someone that can move easily.

(page 17)

1	A	**21** Add 4 to each number: 5 (+ 4), 9 (+ 4), 13 (+ 4), 17 (+ 4), 21.
2	C	**16** Subtract 4 from 16 until you reach 4 (16 (–4), 12 (–4), 8 (–4), 4). Add 4 to repeat pattern: 4 (+ 4), 8 (+ 4), 12 (+ 4), 16.
3	D	**117** Add 8 after each number in line. First, third and fifth numbers: 72 (+ 8), 80 (+ 8), 88; second, fourth and sixth numbers: 101 (+8), 109 (+8), 117.
4	A	**17** Alternate even numbers and odd numbers: (12, 14, 16, 18) and (11, 13, 15, 17). You can also subtract one number from the even numbers to get the odd numbers, eg 12-1 = 11.
5	C	**22** Subtract 2 for first, third and fifth numbers: 38 (–2), 36 (–2), 34 (–2), 32; add 2 for second, fourth and sixth numbers: 16 (+ 2), 18 (+ 2), 20 (+ 2), 22.

Reading Question (page 17)

1	C	Isla does the fewest things. She does one ride: Isla goes on the rollercoaster. Meena goes on the big wheel, the water slide and the dodgem cars. Josh goes on the rollercoaster and the dodgem cars. Dan goes on the rollercoaster and the water slide.

Practice Paper 1B: Mathematics and Non-verbal Reasoning

Mathematics (pages 19–24)

1	E	**413,607** The number is made up of 400,000, 13,000, 600 and 7, which are put together to give 413,607.
2	A	**140ml** 0.2 l is 200ml, so 340ml – 200ml = 140ml.
3	C	**24,214 > 24,2124** The thousands digits are the same but there are 2 hundreds in 24,214 compared to 1 hundred in 24,124.
4	B	**be odd.** The example 1 + 3 + 7 = 11 rules out all options except 'be odd'. All other sums of three odd numbers are also odd.
5	E	**72** 12 × 6 = 72 and 9 × 8 = 72
6	C	**6 Apples:** 7 × 55p = £3.85. £6.25 – £3.85 = £2.40. £2.40 ÷ 40p = 6 pears
7	D	**2012** M = 1000, X = 10, I = 1, so MM = 2000, X = 10 and II = 2, which gives 2012.
8	A	**–185**
9	C	**Harbin** has the greatest temperature difference at 12°C.
10	E	**3.45kg** 400g + 750g + 1500g + 600g + 200g = 3450g = 3.45kg
11	C	**19** Two-thirds like swimming, so one-third do not. One third of 57 is 19 children (57 ÷ 3).
12	D	**15** £3.25 × 15 = £48.75 and £3.25 x 14 = £45.50, so 15 weeks are enough, but 14 or fewer weeks are not.
13	E	**32cm²** The dark shaded triangle that forms part of the parallelogram can be moved to the right-hand side to form a rectangle. Longest side of the shaded rectangle = 11cm – 3cm = 8cm Area = 8cm × 4cm = 32cm²
14	C	**nearest 1000** 476,000 is a multiple of 1000. For the other answers: rounding to the nearest 10 gives 475,680 rounding to the nearest 100 gives 475,700 rounding to the nearest 10,000 gives 480,000, and rounding to the nearest 100,000 gives 500,000.
15	B	**Red knot** Writing all of the numbers using digits makes them easier to compare. The red knot flies the shortest distance at 145,000km.
16	B	**85%** $\frac{34}{40} \times 100 = 85\%$ This could also be calculated by working out 34 × 2.5 because there are two and half times 40 in 100, so multiplying 34 by 2.5 gives the percentage.
17	A	**19.4km** 6.1km + 3.7km + 5km + 4.6km = 19.4km
18	D	**17** 0 goals × 2 games = 0 goals 1 goal × 4 games = 4 goals 2 goals × 1 game = 2 goals 3 goals × 2 games = 6 goals 4 goals × 0 games = 0 goals 5 goals × 1 game = 5 goals 0 + 4 + 2 + 6 + 0 + 5 = 17 goals overall
19	E	**23** Work backwards using reverse operations: 16 – 7 = 9 9 × 2 = 18 18 + 5 = 23 Check by working forwards: (23 – 5) ÷ 2 + 7 = 16
20	A	**20cm** There is no way of making a rectangle perimeter of 20cm with an area of 36cm². (The other answers are possible for these rectangles: B 18cm × 2cm, C 36cm × 1cm, D 12cm × 3cm, E 9cm × 4cm)
21	D	**3** $\frac{3}{12} + \frac{1}{3} = \frac{7}{12}$
22	C	**10.05am** 60km per hour is the same as 1km per minute. 8.20am plus 40 minutes = 9.00am 9.00am plus 60 minutes = 10.00am 10.00am plus 5 minutes = 10.05am

23	E	**63** $1.5 \times 6 = 9$
		$5 \times 1.4 = 7$
		$9 = ? \div 7$
		$9 = 63 \div 7$
24	D	**(5, 4)**
25	B	**2** There are two triangles separated by three rectangles.

Non-verbal Reasoning: Codes (pages 25–27)

1	E	**LY** The first letter indicates the number of triangles in the pattern.
		The second letter indicates the type of shading used in the right-hand triangle.
		L is four triangles and Y is diagonal shading.
2	B	**ET** The first letter indicates the number of small L shapes.
		The second letter indicates the orientation of the crossed lines.
		E is one L shape and T is vertical orientation.
3	D	**MUG** The first letter indicates the outer shape.
		The second letter indicates the proportion of the shape that is shaded.
		The third letter indicates the type of shading.
		M is a circle, U is half of the shape and G is solid black shading.
4	C	**LMO** The first letter indicates the two shapes to the left and right of the shape in the centre.
		The second letter indicates the shape in the centre.
		The third letter indicates the shading of the shape in the centre.
		L is two squares either side of the centre, M is a square in the centre and O is black shading of the shape in the centre.
5	A	**XS** The first letter indicates the number of lines around the edge.
		The second letter indicates the number of crosses.
		X is three lines and S is one cross.
6	A	**EF** The first letter indicates the arrow direction.
		The second letter indicates the size of the triangle.
		E is a north-east pointing arrow and F is a large triangle.
7	D	**SA** The first letter indicates the style of the arrowhead.
		The second letter indicates the number of loops.
		S is a triangular arrowhead and A is one loop.
8	B	**ZM** The first letter indicates the direction of the straight line.
		The second letter indicates the direction of the swirl.
		Z is a north-west pointing line and M is an anticlockwise swirl.
9	B	**IVB** The first letter indicates the line style of the X.
		The second letter indicates the position of the triangle.
		The third letter indicates the type of shading used in the triangle.
		I is a dashed line X, V is the triangle in the bottom section of the X and B is the triangle shaded black.
10	C	**RK** The first letter indicates the type of shading used in the triangle.
		The second letter indicates the position of the white circle.
		R is a black triangle and K is a white circle on the left corner of the triangle.
11	E	**TX** The first letter indicates the outer shape.
		The second letter indicates the line style inside the shape.
		T is a rectangle and X is a wavy line.
12	A	**PBF** The first letter indicates the shape at the bottom of the shield shape.
		The second letter indicates the shape at the top of the shield shape.
		The third letter indicates the number of crosses.
		P is a pointed bottom, B is a curved top and F is three crosses.
13	C	**LW** The first letter indicates the type of shading used in the triangle.
		The second letter indicates the line pattern inside the rectangle.
		L is diagonal shading and W is a diagonal line running from bottom left to top right.

Series (pages 28–30)

1	D	The arrow moves 90° clockwise and an additional line is added to the tail each time.
2	A	The small black square moves clockwise inside the large square. A black dot appears in the small square where the small black square appeared previously, and then the black dots are gradually joined up.
3	C	The outer shape alternates between a rectangle and a circle. The triangle alternates between point up and point down. The shading rotates 45° each time.
4	B	The arrow moves one section anticlockwise each time, and the shaded section moves two sections clockwise each time.
5	E	The curved lines around the edge of the large square replace the straight edges of the small square one at a time, working clockwise. A small line is added to the centre each time.
6	B	The outer shape alternates between a circle and a square and increases in size: small circle, small square, medium circle, medium square, large circle. Each time the shape size increases, all sections of the shape are split in half with the addition of one or more full length lines. The lines remain in the same orientation for a shape type throughout the question.
7	A	The shape rotates 90° anticlockwise each time. There are three types of arrowhead that appear in sequence. There are 3, 2, 1, 2, 3 parallel lines in the sequence.
8	D	The shape with the dot is halved and shaded in the next picture in the sequence.
9	C	The large arrow pointing into the corner moves 90° clockwise each time and alternates between a black and white arrowhead. The small arrow moves clockwise around the square, alternating between being parallel with a side of the square and being diagonal across a corner.
10	E	There is one more black square, one more cross and one fewer white circle each time.
11	B	The pattern alternates between anticlockwise and clockwise. Two lines are added each time.
12	A	The shape rotates 90° anticlockwise each time.
13	B	The two shapes that are at either end of the central arrow swap places. The position of the arrow doesn't follow a pattern.

Practice Paper 2A: English and Verbal Reasoning

English: Roman Writers (pages 32 and 41–42)

1	A	The main purpose of part 1 is to introduce the importance of Roman writing and famous Roman writers.
2	C	'Virgil was born and brought up in a small village in northern Italy.' His early poems were inspired by the farmers and peasants in the area where he lived.
3	D	It is not true that Virgil wanted his poem to be published after he had died. He 'requested that the whole poem was to be burned after his death'.
4	B	The line 'My father is a fly: you can't keep anything secret from him; he's always buzzing around' is a metaphor. It directly compares his father's actions to a fly's actions. Most metaphors have 'is' before the comparison: 'My father is a fly'.
5	D	Pliny the Younger wrote an eyewitness account of the 'volcanic eruption of Mount Vesuvius in AD79'.
6	E	Pliny the Younger's uncle successfully gave the impression of being cheerful for his nervous friend. Pliny thought he was brave because he hid his own fear from his friend.
7	A	The word 'droves' in line 19 has a similar meaning to 'masses'. 'People would come in **droves**…'.
8	B	The word 'insight' in line 28 has a similar meaning to 'understanding'. 'Pliny offers an interesting **insight** into the remarkable character of his uncle.'
9	E	'Roman', 'Italy', *The Aeneid*, 'Mount Vesuvius', 'Pliny the Elder' are all proper nouns. Proper nouns are specific/special names for a person, place, title or thing. 'Roman' is a specific name given to people who came from Ancient Rome/Italy. 'Italy' and 'Mount Vesuvius' are names of places. *The Aeneid* is the title of Virgil's epic poem. 'Pliny the Elder' is the specific name of a well-known Roman.
10	A	There is one adverb in this sentence: '**Luckily**, Emperor Augustus intervened and *The Aeneid* was saved for generations to read and enjoy.'

Punctuation (page 43)

1	C	A semicolon is needed between 'cancelled' and 'the'. It shows two clauses whose ideas are linked, but each clause can independently stand alone.
2	N	No mistake
3	D	An exclamation mark is needed to show excitement in Thea's voice: "We've won the national championship!"
4	C	A comma is needed to separate items in a list of vegetables: 'potatoes, leeks and carrots…'.
5	C	A hyphen is needed between 'chocolate' and 'covered'. We use a hyphen for compound adjectives that go before a noun: 'chocolate-covered raisins'.
6	D	A capital letter is needed for the 'i' in 'islands'. It is part of the proper noun name of a place: 'Shetland Islands'.
7	B	Speech marks are needed at the start of the dialogue sentence: "The volcano is on the verge of erupting."
8	A	A contraction apostrophe is needed to form the correct contraction: 'Don't'.

Spelling (page 44)

1	A	**happily** With adjectives ending in '-y', we replace the 'y' with 'i' and then add '-ly' to change them into adverbs: 'happy – happ + i + ly'.
2	C	**myth** We use 'y' for the sound 'i' in 'myth'.
3	B	**committee** There are three double letters in 'committee': 'mm', 'tt', 'ee'.
4	N	**No mistake**
5	A	**desert** This is the correct spelling for a hot, sandy expanse of land. 'Dessert' is its near homophone. It means a sweet dish in a meal.
6	D	**stomach** This word has an ancient Greek origin. The 'ch' sound at the end of the word has a 'k' sound.
7	C	**fourth** For an ordinal number word, we add 'th' to the end of 'four'.
8	D	**potatoes** We add 'es' for the plural of potato.

Grammar (page 45)

1	B	**would have** We use 'would have' to talk about something that could have happened in the past but then did not happen.
2	C	**her** The possessive pronoun. It tells us that Queen Dhanya owned the stallion.
3	A	**best** The other four words are not grammatically correct. 'Best' is a superlative adjective and does not need 'est', 'er', 'most'.
4	B	**is taken** We use 'is taken' to show an action of something that happens regularly (in the past, present and future). We use 'is' for a singular noun – the recycling bin.
5	D	**funniest** This is a superlative adjective. For adjectives ending in '-y', we replace the 'y' with an 'i' before we add '-est': funn + i + est.
6	E	**an** We add the article 'an' before words starting in a vowel – 'an unusual insect'.
7	C	**before** This is a time conjunction. 'Before' is the only example in the list of conjunctions that makes sense when Zoe baked the fruit muffins.

Verbal Reasoning (page 46)

1	B	**TOO** The climber sTOOd on top of the mountain peak. The other three letter choices do not make proper words or give a wrong subject–verb agreement or do not make sense in a sentence.
2	D	**OWL** My dog often grOWLs at my friend's cat. The other three letter choices do not make proper words or do not make sense in a sentence.
3	C	**SIT** The Duke's ancient castle is now open to viSITors. The other three letter choices do not make proper words.
4	B	**BED** The servant girl was expected to be oBEDient. The other three letter choices do not make sense.
5	E	**KEY** Watch out for that hocKEY stick! The other three letter choices do not make sense.

(page 47)

1	B	**ON** The counting pattern for the set of pairs is + 3 (H–K), –1 (K–J), + 3 (J–M), –1 (M–L), + 3 (L–O), –1 (O–N). Start each pair with the last letter from the previous pair.
2	B	**YB** First letters in pairs go forwards one letter from U (U, V, W, X, Y); second letters in pairs go back one letter from F (F, E, D, C, B).
3	E	**PN** First, third and fifth pairs – alphabetical order forwards from EF (EF, GH, IJ); second, fourth and sixth pairs – count two letters backwards from V (V–T, S–Q, P–N).
4	D	**UR** The counting pattern is + 1, –1, + 2, –2, + 3, –3. AB (count 1 letter forward); ZY (count 1 letter backwards); CE (count 2 letters forward); XV (count 2 letters backwards); FI (count 3 letters forward); UR (count 3 letters backwards).
5	A	**HJ** The counting pattern is + 5, + 2. The first letters in the pairs are in alphabetical order from C (C, D, E, F, G, H). The second letters in the pairs are as follows: First pair: count + 5 letters from C (C–H); Second pair: count + 2 letters forward (D–F); third pair: count + 5 letters from E (E–J); fourth pair: count + 2 letters from F (F–H); fifth pair: count + 5 letters from G (G–L); sixth pair: count + 2 letters from H (H–J).

(page 48)

1	A	**s** Two new words are 'port and 'yaks'. Move 's' in first word. Add to the end of the second word.
2	B	**n** Two new words are 'sack' and 'town'. Move 'n' in first word. Add to the end of the second word.
3	E	**e** Two new words are 'quit' and 'robe'. Move 'e' in first word. Add to the end of the second word.
4	E	**e** Two new words are 'rang' and 'made'. Move 'e' in the first word. Add to the end of the second word.
5	B	**h** Two new words are 'sell' and 'hitch'. Move 'h' in the first word. Add at the beginning of the second word.

(page 49)

1	B	**plot** (plan conspire): to work out an idea or action; (land allotment): an area of ground to build or garden on.
2	C	**poor** (needy penniless): to lack in money; (sub-standard dismal): bad quality.
3	E	**notice** (observe spot): to see someone or something; (poster advertisement): written information or announcement.
4	A	**break** (crack shatter): to be damaged by a strong force; (interval playtime): to have a rest from a main activity.
5	C	**drive** (steer operate): to control a machine/vehicle; (determination ambition): the desire to succeed.

(page 50)

1	B	**p** The four words are: flap, push, trap, pear.	fla(p)ush	tra(p)ear
2	C	**d** The four words are: gold, drop, head, down.	gol(d)rop	hea(d)own
3	D	**n** The four words are: basin, nudge, widen, note.	basi(n)udge	wide(n)ote
4	E	**w** The four words are: slow, wood, allow, wand.	slo(w)ood	allo(w)and
5	A	**y** The four words are: sky, yell, handy, yellow.	sk(y)ell	hand(y)ellow

(page 51)

1	E	**20** $59 - 7 = 32 + 20$ $(59 - 7 = 52)$ $(32 + \mathbf{20} = 52)$
2	C	**3** $7 \times 3 + 12 = 10 \times 3 + 3$ $(7 \times 3\ (21) + 12 = 33)$ $(10 \times 3\ (30) + \mathbf{3} = 33)$
3	D	**4** $48 \div 8 \times 4 = 5 \times 4 + 4$ $(48 \div 8\ (6) \times 4 = 24)$ $(5 \times \mathbf{4}\ (20) + 4 = 24)$

Reading Question (page 51)

1	B	The sentence 'Jaden is a stronger swimmer than Thea' is true:
		Thea can definitely swim 25m.
		Jaden can definitely swim 50m.
		A and D: The information does not tell us how far or fast Antoni can swim.
		There is no information to tell us if sentences C and E are true.

Practice Paper 2B: Mathematics and Non-verbal Reasoning

Mathematics (pages 53–58)

1	C	**98**
2	B	**$5\frac{1}{2}$** $3 \div 4 = \frac{3}{4}$ $\frac{3}{4} + 2 = 2\frac{3}{4}$ $2\frac{3}{4} \times 2 = 5\frac{1}{2}$
3	B	**2688** $842 + 1169 + 677 = 2688$
4	D	**8** There are 14 banana symbols in total, so each represents 8 bananas, as $112 \div 14 = 8$.
5	A	**6.5** 6.47 is between 6.4 and 6.5, and is closer to 6.5 than 6.4.
6	B	**£2 + £1 + 50p + 10p + 5p + 1p** $£10 - £6.34 = £3.66$ change $£2 + £1 + 50p + 10p + 5p + 1p = £3.66$
7	B	For B, there will be two overlapping squares on one face and no square on the opposite face.
8	E	**17** This is a sequence of consecutive prime numbers.
9	A	**11** Work backwards: $63 \div 9 = 7$ successful plants each with 9 strawberries 7 successful + 4 eaten = 11 plants originally
10	E	**−9°C** $4°C - 13°C = -9°C$
11	D	**119°** $180° - 125° = 55°$ $180° - 55° - 64° = 61°$ $180° - 61° = 119°$
12	C	**£238** $£280 \div 10 = £28$ (calculate 10%) $£28 \div 2 = £14$ (calculate 5%) $£28 + £14 = £42$ (calculate 15%) $£280 - £42 = £238$
13	A	**18** It is a multiple of 2 and 3 but NOT a multiple of 4.
14	D	**3** $10, 8\frac{1}{4}, 6\frac{1}{2}, 4\frac{3}{4}, 3$
15	B	**26m** Each long edge of the fence is $1m + 8.5m + 1m = 10.5m$ The short edge of the fence is $1m + 3m + 1m = 5m$ $10.5m + 10.5m + 5m = 26m$
16	B	**25 minutes** 0.2 litres is the same as 200ml. 200ml is five times 40ml. So 200ml takes 5×5 minutes = 25 minutes
17	D	**$2.56 + 2.44 = 5$**
18	D	**144cm²** $12cm \times 12cm = 144cm^2$

19	E	**70m** 20m (above sea level) + 50m (below sea level) = 70m
20	B	**6** Factors of 42: 1, 2, 3, 6, 7, 14, 21 and 42
		Factors of 90: 1, 2, 3, 5, 6, 9, 10, 15, 18, 30, 45 and 90
21	C	**101 minutes** 12:42 to 13:00 is 18 minutes
		13:00 to 14:00 is 60 minutes
		14:00 to 14:23 is 23 minutes
		18 + 60 + 23 = 101 minutes
22	D	**(5, 2)**
23	A	**58** Friday 9 July to Saturday 31 July = 23 days
		Sunday 1 August to Tuesday 31 August = 31 days
		Wednesday 1 September to Sunday 4 December = 4 days
		23 + 31 + 4 = 58 days
24	C	**45** 540 ÷ 12 = 45
25	D	2 pairs of parallel lines: 1 pair of perpendicular lines:

Non-verbal Reasoning: Like Figures (pages 59–61)

1	B	Each shape is white, made up of straight lines and has a small white circle at one vertex.
2	B	Each circle is divided into six equal sectors; one is shaded black, two are white, one has dots, one has horizontal shading and the other has diagonal shading.
3	B	All have three shapes with two separately overlapping the shape in the middle.
4	D	Each shape has either two triangles on one side of the wavy line and one semicircle on the other side, or two semicircles on one side and one triangle on the other.
5	C	Each shape is made up of three squares and one rectangle.
6	D	Each shape is a quadrilateral with two black dots. The black dots are positioned on separate, adjoining lines.
7	E	Each outer shape has a smaller version of itself inside and horizontally reflected. The larger outer shape also contains any shape that is small and black.
8	B	Each shape contains two thicker lines that are joined at one end and form a 90° angle, together with three thinner lines.
9	B	Each shape has only one line of symmetry.
10	A	The total number of sides in each group of shapes is twelve.
11	A	Each shape is split exactly in half. One half contains two crosses.
12	C	Each large white shape is accompanied by two smaller versions of the shape, one shaded black that is overlapped by the large shape and one with horizontal striped shading that overlaps the large shape.
13	E	All are made up of four small shapes: two squares, one triangle and one circle. One square is always black and the other square always has vertical striped shading.

Analogies (pages 62–64)

1	C	The short lines at the vertices of the large shape change into smaller versions of the large shape.
2	B	The smallest, inner shape becomes the largest, outer shape and the other two shapes reduce in size. Each shape retains its shading.
3	E	The shape is rotated through 180°.
4	C	The solid lines become dashed lines and a reflection in a vertical line completes the shape with solid lines.
5	A	The second shape is the overlapping parts of the first shape.
6	A	The left-hand shape rotates 90° anticlockwise and the right-hand shape rotates 180°. The black/white shading is reversed.
7	D	The number of circles in the first shape becomes the number of sides of the second shape. The number of dots becomes the number of crosses.
8	B	The shape at the top of the line is moved to the right of the line. The shape at the bottom of the line is rotated 90° anticlockwise and added to the top of the line.
9	B	The shape is reduced in size and rotated 90° anticlockwise.
10	E	The line thickness is reduced and one more side added to the shape.
11	C	The 'T' shapes overlap and the line patterns are combined.
12	A	White shapes remain unchanged, black shapes change to triangles and striped shapes change to circles.
13	C	Starting with the top left arrow and moving clockwise, each arrow is repeated the same number of times as the number of small lines crossing the arrow.